Paul Durcan was born in Dublin in 1944, of Co. Mayo parents. He studied Archaeology and Medieval History at University College Cork. In 1974 he won the Patrick Kavanagh Award and he received Creative Writing Bursaries from the Arts Council of Ireland in 1976 and 1980. He has given readings of his poems throughout the world. In 1981 he represented Ireland at the Struga Poetry Festival in Yugoslavia and in 1983 undertook a tour of the Soviet Union at the invitation of the Union of Soviet Writers. He is a member of Aosdána.

Among Durcan's other published works are:

Endsville (with Brian Lynch), New Writers Press, Dublin, 1967
O Westport in the Light of Asia Minor, Anna Livia Press, Dublin, 1975
Teresa's Bar, Gallery Press, Dublin, 1976
Sam's Cross, Profile Press, Dublin, 1978
Jesus, Break His Fall, Raven Arts Press, Dublin, 1980
Ark of the North, Raven Arts Press, Dublin, 1982
Jumping the Train Tracks with Angela, Raven Arts Press, Dublin/Carcanet New Press, Manchester, 1983
The Berlin Wall Café, Blackstaff Press, Belfast, 1985 (Poetry Book Society Choice).
Going Home to Russia, Blackstaff Press, Belfast, 1987

The Selected
Paul Durcan

edited by Edna Longley

THE
BLACKSTAFF
PRESS

BELFAST

First published in 1982
by The Blackstaff Press Limited
with the assistance of The Arts Council of Northern Ireland

Second edition 1985
Reprinted 1986, 1987, 1988
The Blackstaff Press Limited
3 Galway Park, Dundonald, Belfast BT16 0AN

Printed in Northern Ireland
by Belfast Litho Printers Limited

British Library Cataloguing in Publication Data
Durcan, Paul
The selected Paul Durcan. — 2nd ed.
I. Title   II. Longley, Edna
821'.914   PR6054.U72

Library of Congress Cataloging-in-Publication Data
Durcan, Paul, 1944–
The selected Paul Durcan.
Includes indexes.
I. Longley, Edna.   II Title
PR6054.U72A6   1985   821'.914   85–20082

ISBN 0-85640-354-7

to
Nessa
and
Sarah and Síabhra

Contents

from *Teresa's Bar*

from *Sam's Cross*

from *Jesus, Break His Fall*

Introduction

The titles of Paul Durcan's four full collections – O *Westport in the Light of Asia Minor, Teresa's Bar, Sam's Cross* and *Jesus, Break His Fall* – cover both the visionary and the Irish aspects of his poetry. They also imply a likely friction between the two; since Sam's Cross was the birthplace of the murdered Michael Collins, while 'Teresa's Bar' represents an antidote to all the hurts and constraints of society:

> But Teresa deep down had no time for time
> Or for those whose business has to do with time .

Durcan is visionary, first of all, in his faith. This faith extends to literature itself, as when he salutes a significant Trinity of writers:

> I have not 'met' God, I have not 'read'
> David Gascoyne, James Joyce, or Patrick Kavanagh:
> I believe in them.

Durcan's own work achieves extra-literary qualities too, if occasionally at the expense of certain literary ones. His 'mystical entrances' affirm lost Edens, like Ireland 'Before the Celtic Yoke', or an ideal peaceable kingdom: 'Even the grey pools by the bridge cannot help / But be motherfathers to wildflowers' ('Letter to Ben, 1972'). But such visions, including more personal oases of love, are often hard-won from time, space, and the potential destructiveness of all relationships within the human family. Durcan gives the name 'Love in a Grave' to the long summing-up poem that concludes *Sam's Cross* (it proved difficult to excerpt for this selection, as did his recent sequence, *Ark of the North*). The poet cannot always make himself 'the middle of it all' ('The Nun's Bath'); and 'She Mends an Ancient Wireless' inscribes a characteristic imaginative profile:

From my tiny perch I cry once more your praises
And call out your name across the great divide – Nessa.

Even when celebratory, Durcan's perceptions have a bizarre aura
which shades into disturbing possibilities. In another love poem
('Hymn to Nessa') the two watchers convey peril as well as intensity:

I looked back and saw her wave towards me
She burned through her eyes
I looked back and saw her wave towards me
Her face burning in coals

Although surrealistic or fantastic effects may underline the oneness
of phenomena – all the hats of humanity in 'The Hat Factory' – they
chiefly strike discords: the refrain uttered by a dying man ('Rider
Haggard, Rider Haggard: / Storm Jameson, Storm Jameson'), the
scenario of 'The Head Transplant', the cosmic strangeness of 'La
Terre des Hommes':

Fancy meeting *you* out here in the desert:
Hallo Clockface.

Surrealism is also Durcan's most powerful satirical weapon,
crystallising incongruities between the ideal and the actual. 'Two
History Professors' take a questioning West Indian at his word when
he complains 'They are using a bacon-slicer on my mind'. In
'Charlie's Mother', a different agent of Irish orthodoxy acquires
Dali-esque solidity:

Brendan, does *your* mother have a hold over *you*?
Mine does over *me*. I keep beseeching her
To take her purple-veined hand out of my head. . .

Satire is perhaps too cool and intellectual a term for such poems. It
might be truer to say that Durcan's negatives fiercely invert his
positives: that his vision encompasses dreams and nightmares.

As regards specific attacks on Irish society, Durcan continues
where Patrick Kavanagh's crusading zeal ran out. *The Great Hunger*
apart, Kavanagh lampooned Dublin's 'Bohemian Jungle' and the
'devil Mediocrity' from a subjective, too narrowly literary point of
view. Durcan's broadly-based outrage, which sometimes breaks
through his verbal control, indicts the concrete jungle, the Church,
the repression of sex and women, the bourgeoisie, the murder of

bodies and minds. Fiction, if not poetry, may have thoroughly savaged these targets already. However, Durcan is not only peculiarly sensitive to Ireland's changing line-up of anti-life forces, but able to embody them in vivid symbols, portraits and fables. Materialism and the social consequences of expansion provide an area of richly urgent concern. 'Please Stay in the Family Clovis' and 'The Day of the Starter', for instance, illustrate how maternal and marital affection can become confused with curtains, cutlery and cars. 'Tullynoe: Tête-à-Tête in the Parish Priest's Parlour' sanctifies the confusion:

> '. . . he was a grand man.'
> 'He was: he had the most expensive Toyota you can buy.'
> 'He had: well, it was only beautiful.'

Durcan's naturally religious cast of mind recoils from the Catholic Church's brand of hostility to life and love. Many poems subvert puritanism, while 'Bishop of Cork Murders his Wife' hammers the accepted superiority of violence to sex, and maleness to femaleness. A subtler skit, 'Irish Hierarchy Bans Colour Photography', exploits an appropriate analogy for black-and-white attitudes and stunted awareness. On the other hand, 'Teresa', 'Polycarp' and 'Fat Molly' personify fertile sexuality and sensuality. The latter, a carnal incarnation of Cathleen ní Houlihan and thus another version of primal Ireland, lives 'On the other side of the forest from the monk-fort at Kells'.

Durcan's critique of the South is sharpened by his sense of the North. No other Southern Irish poet has so painfully and continuously responded to the Ulster Troubles. His epigrammatic epitaph 'Ireland 1972' condenses a family heritage of violence, now inexorable:

> Next to the fresh grave of my beloved grandmother
> The grave of my firstlove murdered by my brother.

Five years later things have not changed much, with Durcan portraying himself as an isolated communicator to the deaf:

> 'I've become so lonely, I could die −' he writes,
> The native who is an exile in his native land:
> 'Do you hear me whispering to you across the Golden Vale?
> Do you hear me bawling to you across the hearthrug?'
>
> ('Ireland 1977')

Some of Durcan's whispers take the form of irony – 'National Day of Mourning for 12 Protestants'. Others emphasise that bigotry is not confined to one sect or province ('What is a Protestant, Daddy?'), or function as reminders of the Protestant tradition in the South ('Protestant Old Folks' Coach Tour', 'The Weeping Headstones of the Isaac Becketts'). Perhaps his quietest and most effective comment is 'The Night They Murdered Boyle Somerville'. An old man, during a train journey that traverses much history and geography, simply remarks:

> 'I found out what was in it, and was not in it,
> The night they murdered Boyle Somerville;
> I knew then that it was only the sky had a roof.'

Durcan's elegies for victims of all colours more directly proclaim the incompatibility of murder with all he holds dear:

> You made music, and that was all: You were realists –
> And beautiful were your feet.
>
> ('In Memory: The Miami Showband:
> Massacred 31 July 1975')

Durcan's alternative Ireland not only includes 'Desire under the steeples and spires', and excludes terrorism, but must be fit for his heroes and heroines. The diverse integrity of his real-life idols is matched by the idiosyncrasies of his invented models: Teresa, Polycarp, Fat Molly, 'The Kilfenora Teaboy', Constance Purfield who 'prefers the trees', 'Nora and Hilda', 'The County Engineer' and his wife. In this truly human family, makers of love not war, there is compassionate room for marginal and ambiguous figures like 'The Butterfly Collector of Corofin'. Durcan can characterise with names alone: 'Gogo's Late Wife Tranquilla'. And the fictional names of his heterogeneous dramatis personae interact oddly with actual placenames: this contributes to the shifting projection of the country's real features against a Platonic conception. Durcan has named more places than most Irish poets. He sometimes just states and hates middle Ireland – 'I've Got the Drimoleague Blues' – but generally placenames become 'magic passwords into eternity' ('Going Home to Mayo, Winter, 1949'). In 'Birth of a Coachman' implicit resonance creates the 'magic' of a more hopeful symbolic journey than that of 'The Night They Murdered Boyle Somerville':

Praising the breasts of the hills round Port Laoise;
Sailing full furrow through the Curragh of Kildare,
Through the thousand sea-daisies of a thousand white sheep. . .

These richly textured lines evince an open Romanticism rare in contemporary poetry. Their obvious assonance raises the ghost of Gaelic metre, but the Irishness of Durcan's language depends more on conversational idiom – for example, the pervasive 'used [to]' – and its various rhetorical extensions, such as the amplified sentence ('The Hat Factory', 'Birth of a Coachman'), or a stately elaboration:

. . .while the cradle is but a grave
The grave is not a cradle but is for ever. . .
And I see that all church-architecture is but coiffure
And all mystical entrances are through women's faces.

                                                    ('Phoenix Park Vespers')

No loader of every rift with ore, though capable of startling concentration, Durcan resembles D.H. Lawrence in his tendency to write 'the poetry of the present moment', or adopt a biblical style of prophecy. But while some poems over-saturate their subjects – some titles nearly exhaust them! – he can also renew the simplest ballad-forms. 'Backside to the Wind', which wistfully imagines 'a French Ireland', combines an old air with a down-to-earth refrain:

Yet I have no choice but to leave, to leave,
And yet there is nowhere I more yearn to live
Than in my own wild countryside,
Backside to the wind.

That quatrain might exemplify the way in which Paul Durcan's poetry seems in touch with the deepest wells of native Irish sensibility, yet radically challenges their pollution. In addition to his other achievements, he has developed the conscience of the race.

Edna Longley

Animus Anima Amen

He went into a bar, fell deeply in love with a strange girl, and said:

> Where did you come from?
> The moon.
> I bet *he* didn't like that.
> Who?
> Him.
> Who's him?
> The man –
> In the bloody moon. Why didn't you say so?
> Katherine.
> Paul.

And he smiled. And she smiled. And they relaxed in each other's arms for about a year or so. In the end, she went back to the fellow in the bloody moon.

Outside the Descent of the Holy Ghost

Hosanna to the young woman in the long black rain coat
Ascending the church steps on an afternoon in winter;
I did not doubt the deliberation with which she weaved
A sensual path into the black shadows of the porch
And yet how frail a creature
That now was minutely flying headlong into the Wall of God.

But I had but two eyes on her, for behind me
Between the sunlight and the snow
Came a small family out for their Sunday walk;
A family just like any other family
Except for the Alsatian dog prancing beside them:
Geoffrey, I heard them call, Geoffrey, Geoffrey.

Now safe from that small family for a time at least
I think of you – young woman on the church steps –
Of how families are made – or not made –
Of how I am my daughters' father and I pray
May they not inherit the world of the family
And the murderous animal of possession.
Dear nameless woman, suntrap, scarp of snow,
If you should see the hawthorn blossom on a day in winter
Relish the actuality, do not flinch from pain.

Letter to Ben, 1972

4 The Terrace, At The Ridge of The Two Air-Demons, Co. Leitrim

It is half-past nine on a July night;
The town's, and the emperor's, artillery are outside,
Are all perched up inside an ocean wave that's riding
– Alongwith the weed-adorned boards of sunlight, filthy jewels and
          millefiori refuse –
Seabreezes that themselves are riding into each other at right angles
Across this broken street we call *The Terrace;*
And there is grass growing in the sand and old Ben
Is stretched out happily in a sunny corner too – never again
Will he or I be a cause of fright to each other;
We're on the same side, just different sides of the ocean.

Come on up, Ben, take a seat in the gods,
The roof has at least three-quarters blown off,
Even the grey pools by the bridge cannot help
But be motherfathers to wildflowers
And all the wild animals too, including ourselves, the bear and the
          fox,
Whom tycoons thought to cage,
Have broken grave and cursed no one:
We know the mines will produce in their own time
Abundance:
Iron hills in the east
And gold in the northwest.
Oh such light from the east, Ben,
And it is only half-past nine on a summer's night.
Darkness has entered already the arena
Trampling the manure-larded sand and straw
With all her young splendour more bare and ebony than before;
Her ceremonial chains proclaiming no escape nor for the spectator.
So, in history, the ridge becomes deserted now and then:
Right now, just you and me, Ben, and the species.

Ballina, Co. Mayo

for Sailorson

It is the last town before the river meets the sea.

At evening in summertime young men and old men
Stand on the bridge watching the waters flow under them, under the
    arches;
They lean their elbows on the wall with their hands cupped as if in
    prayer;
But though they may in themselves be kneeling
They are standing squarely on the callous pavement;
The air is full of reasonableness –
If their own faces float past them they are not bothered,
They do not dwell or harp on it;
And if at their life's end they whisper for a priest
It may be because of what they can hear among all these
    waters' silences and sounds
Such as the tiny object that being borne along helplessly upon the
    waters
Is seeming to say: *Let this chalice pass from me. . .*
Or, it should be reported, making the sound that these words make
And, how can we not say, with meaning too.

Poor Splinter trapped in the emotion –

Poem for my Father

I

He could feel, as he lay half-awake on his mat,
Not knowing if it were night or day,
The same black space behind the ears,
My nightmare is my family, and these hands of mine
Would wrench off my shoulders if they could,
But I am as the waters of my fate,
My father plunging through them to become me.

Outside, a commuter, refugee, goes leaping along the street
As by his fingertips he clings
To the broken glass of a late winter twilight sky.
Marked man, face up against the sky,
Riddled with aspirations.

II

I saw through my fingers a man in the sky
Moving out the bay:

Reality's Jack swaying out to sea.

What need to look back
Into the night at the root of it?
Who grips the twine to a poor man's kite
Grips me.

The Nun's Bath

I drink to the middle of it all.
Between the sandhills,
The sandhills between the hayfields and the sea,
There stood a tub and in it
A buxom nun who scrubbed herself as if
The early morning air was itself the water,
A water dance that was being wound
Round her by a yellow duck.

Now here in this gruesome London pub
I make myself the middle of it all.
I know that when I stand to get my beer
Another nomad may well steal my stool;
And let the barmaid be mournful if she will.
My job is to be present which I am.
There is the day ahead with more or less agony
Than to suffer all day in the Convent of Mercy.

They Say the Butterfly is the Hardest Stroke

for Richard Riordan

From coves below the cliffs of the years
I have dipped into *Ulysses*,
A Vagrant, Tarry Flynn –
But for no more than ten minutes or a page;
For no more than to keep in touch
With minds kindred in their romance with silence.
I have not 'met' God, I have not 'read'
David Gascoyne, James Joyce, or Patrick Kavanagh:
I believe in them.
Of the song of him with the world in his care
I am content to know the air.

November 1967

to Katherine

I awoke with a pain in my head
And my mother standing at the end of the bed;
'There's bad news in the paper,' she said
'Patrick Kavanagh is dead.'

After a week which was not real
At last I settled down to a natural meal;
I was sitting over a pint and a beef sandwich
In Mooney's across the street from the Rotunda.

By accident I happened to tune in
To the conversation at the table from me;
I heard an old Northsider tell to his missus
'He was pure straight; God rest him; not like us.'

General Vallancey's Waltz

for A.K.

I'm a Westmeath solicitor long lost in Peking, long, lost, and
        forgotten,
And I used sit up in my hall late into the night listening for *you;*
But it was not enough, it was not enough,
So I sailed up the Liffey from China,
Back to the wall, back to the wall,
To Liberty Hall.

I got married in due course, to a good Peking lass, of good
        Communist stock,
But she turned turkey on me, said she needed more money,
That there was not enough, that there was not enough,
So I sailed up the Liffey from China,
Back to the wall, back to the wall,
To Liberty Hall.

Oh forgive me my shout if I fall through your easy chair, through the
        back of your easy chair,
My knees are the crux of the world's local problem, no knees – no
        heaven;
Oh but there *is* all in all, there *is* all in all,
So I sailed up the Liffey from China,
Back to the wall, back to the wall,
To Liberty Hall.

The Daughters Singing to their Father

Now he will grope back into the abode and crouch down;
Another dry holocaust in the urban complex over;
Over another stagger home along the semi-detached gauntlet;
Another day done. It has never not been,
Not even on worse days when only grave-dark was craved for.
He will crouch down and whether the night
Be starry or not
He will behold no stillness take shape upon his knees;
Nor rainbow book nor snow-white cat;
Nor will that woman of women, fire of fires,
            – the one of the old smile
Breaking out in sheet gold in her cave-red hair –
Hover near, nor turn the page over
For her votary in the broken chair.
No matter what bedlam or vacuum the night may rear
He will hear only his daughters singing to him
From behind the arabic numerals of the clock:
'There is no going back, boy, there is no going back.'
Long will he gaze into the clock, and to that last spouse
Under the skyline – for his daughters give thanks.

La Terre des Hommes

Fancy meeting *you* out here in the desert:
Hallo Clockface.

Aughawall Graveyard

Lonely lonely lonely lonely:
The story with a middle only.

Ireland 1972

Next to the fresh grave of my beloved grandmother
The grave of my firstlove murdered by my brother.

O Westport in the Light of Asia Minor

I

Feet crossed, arms behind his head,
God lay below the skyline hidden from sight;
And Gauloise smoke trailed up the sky.

British frocks and dresses lay draped on the rocks,
Gray flashing windows of a nineteenth-century boutique,
While on the sands the girls lay lazily on their sides
All moon in the daylight
Musing 'What is he like?' but at the back of their mind
The heart raged on:
Flame seamed with all the scorn of a soldier
Saying 'After the battle'.

II

But often the Reek would stand with a cloud round its head;
Behind the sky stood God with a cleaver raised;
Yet when cocky men peered round the curtain of sky
There was no god and the mists came,
Lay down on the West coast,
Fur off the back of a graveyard,
As though an ape had got the tedium of a thousand years between his
        maulers
And shoved it across the world onto our land:
The mists put the fear of our mother into us:
I am what I am for fear of hiding in the action
And yet —

If this world is not simply atmosphere pierced through and through
With the good doubt,
Then here it was Red Riding Hood who was laid up in bed;
It was Red-Eared Black Tongue who crouched at the bedside;
And she did the child no harm but good.

But there were some who had guts, took action and stayed;

And standing on the mountains of their dread saw
The islands come up through the mists
– Seductive garments that a man would dream of –
And with the islands finally the sun;
Black at the edges, pure red at the centre.

They came at a run down the mountain
Landing with such falls that even the few small hard gold pieces in
     their pockets
Smashed into pieces so infinitesimal that not even a Shylock ever
     would find them;
They came starting out of their breeches out onto the stoney shore,
The sea was a great unnamed flower whose leaves they stood under
And danced to ring upon ring;
Thin prickly bearded men casting ridiculousness to the multitude,
Casting it in great armfuls made bountiful by the slow and graceful
     whirling of their arms
And they sang: As though a rock were naked.

On a June Afternoon in Saint Stephen's Green

With MacDara I found myself walking
Behind a young woman in her light summer wear.
If we were walking, she was riding
The clear waters of her cotton dress
And I thought: had I the choice I had been a woman –
Instead I am strung up on a cloud called mind.
Even were I to walk naked my body were a cumbersome coat.
O fortunate soul, walking on her hips through the Green.

Please Stay in the Family Clovis

Please stay in the family Clovis:
The tawny curtains in the front parlour
– Though we do not use that room –
Would somehow not look quite the same
Without you – when you get married
We could put the presents in the front parlour –
Blankets pillowcases teaspoons carvers –
All in a row on the sideboard:
No better nor more thoughtful present
Than a quality set of carvers Clovis:
Why – you and Olive and (D.V.) your children
Could live here with us:
All it would mean would be a bit more cleaning
And do not snap back that I am only just dreaming:
I'm talking about reality Clovis:
And we still would not have to use the front parlour:
Love Mother.

Phoenix Park Vespers

I

A man hiking the roads or tramping the streets
Has elegies for hills and epitaphs for houses
But his wife, while she has thought only for the ultimate destination
And is much more strict about weekly attendance at church,
Has much less belief in an after-life or in heaven, –
Thus under the conifers of the Phoenix Park,
Under the exceedingly lonely conifers of the Phoenix Park,
Under their blunt cones and amidst their piercing needles,
I squatted down and wept;
I who have but rarely shed a tear in sorrow.
The hurriedly-emptying October evening skies neither affirmed nor
      denied
A metaphysics of sex
But reflected themselves merely in the fields below
As flocks of kindred-groups, courting couples, and footballers,
Old men, and babes, and loving friends,
And youths and maidens gay,
Scattered for homes.
The floor where I crouched was lit-up by litters
Of the terracotta cones
And in the darkness at the heart of the wood
Kids played at giants and gnomes.
A woman (of whom I was so fond I actually told her so),
Not as a question but as a rebuke,
Remarked to me: 'What are you thinking?'
And I knew that whatever I replied she would add
Half-coyly, mockingly, coaxingly:
'Oh my dear little *buachaillín*, but it is all one;
Enough of Baudelaire, there *is* no connection.'

II

I think now of her face as of a clock
With the long hand passing over her eyes
But passing over backwards as well as forwards,
To and fro – like a speedometer needle.
And this long hand, where once was her hound-like nose,
At once tells the time and points a warning finger;
Warning me to bear in mind that while the cradle is but a grave
The grave is not a cradle but is for ever.
And while her iron voice clanks tonelessly away
Her face grows blacker under her heaped-over hair;
And I see that all church-architecture is but coiffure
And all mystical entrances are through women's faces.
She opens her mouth and I step out onto her ice-pink tongue
To be swallowed up for ever in the womb of time.

Dún Chaoin

for Bob, Angela, and Rachel, in Nigeria

I was standing at the counter
In a bar at the world's end.
The large weathered man behind it
Was more native to the place than the place itself.
His father's fathers. . .
A big blue man like that, I thought, could not be strange
With a stranger:
So when he did not speak
An old fear whistled through me:
I am not welcome in this place.
I kept a grip on my pint glass
And my eyes to the left of me
Gripping the bay-window and outside
The red sun at nightfall
In the same plane as the bar room
Descending the window pane.
Its going down took about as long
As it takes a boy or girl to climb down a tree.
Gone and not long after
I thought I could hear
A longlost music long lost from the earth
And as I looked up from the counter shaking my head
The big man too was shaking his, birds and tears
Falling out of the rafters of his eyes. The both of us
Laughed and he turned up the volume
Of his openly concealed battered old wireless,
Telefunken,
And when we were going out he said: Good night
And may God bless you on the road.
I went out willing to sleep on mountainsides anywhere
Fearing no man or beast, machine or mist.

Combe Florey

to Laura Waugh

Wilderness that not always would deliver:
But to us come from the hot clink of London
It was Tel Aviv the hill of Spring and garden of the Sea
To wake in the mornings and to hear the stillness –
And that in spite or because of
The racket of birds – more than one
Woodpecker inhabited the oak outside my window
And at six each morning wound up their clocks in a loud manner
Not to speak of the woodpigeon, the cuckoo, the others
Whose names I do not know.
I said to the woman of the house in my own painful and boulder
        fashion:
It is a crying shame to be a creature of this earth
And not know the names of the birds in the trees
And yet I know the names of fifty motor cars.
She said: Lord, I do not think I know the name of even one of the little
        creatures.
And so saying, she gave tiny feet back to my boulder and pain.

From Gougane Barra into Cork City: Augustine of Hippo Confesses

for Martin Green

I saw the father in the daughter's eyes
And his father's face in his and
I saw the world begin to spin and spin
And when she said: 'I may as well go home'
I said: 'You may as well go home.'

But then when she had gone
The machinery came crashing to a halt
And I was dazed and the table ached
And I was in a cafeteria
Where all the persons at the tables ached:

Ached until it appeared we were being all split up,
And up the aisle in a whisper chanting
Came a black man the nonchalance of whose swerve
Upset me deeply to the roots of the groin
And he was saying: 'I am my memory, I am my memory.'

Brighton Beach

Have you ever watched the sea go out at Brighton
And known that you were not going with it too;
And the gray horizon putting up the shutters
And wished you were behind them long ago?

For it is blue by night in Normandy
And Normans are by morning fairer still
And stick, as they walk out the day at noon,
Red feathers in the yellow fields of time.

Have you ever watched your bare-armed gray-haired mother
And she is in the garden hanging out
Your shirt, and your father's, on the clothes line?
From Brighton that is the horizon that I see.

And on the shore deserted as that room
That every child has to make her own
I stand behind the windows of my eyes
As the sea is blown away by the winding gulls.

Black Sister

Black sister with an afro halo round your head
And a handbag by your side and a string of beads;
Watching for news from a newsreel in the dark
Of the television lounge of a country hotel.
You are lean, tall and fruitful as a young beech
And seductive as the tree of knowledge
But – forgive me but is this not the millennium to inquire? –
Is that not you yourself stepping across the screen
Out of missionary fields into a country courthouse,
Machine-gun firing from your thigh, and freedom
On your dying lips?
But you are whispering to me tonight:
'Oh Acton let us be ambiguous tonight.'

Instead you are cooped up in Ireland in a small hotel
Waiting for your boy whose magic daddy
Though no niggard to mission fields at Sunday Mass
Is not standing for his son to hitch up with a black bitch
Even if she's a Catholic virgin;
She's black; and a whore therefore.
And electric mammy than whom there is no more fiercesome
Drum-beater for black babies
Collapsed when she glimpsed the sun dancing halo round your head.
But you're a patient girl –
While over dark deep well waters lit up by huge arc lights
You whisper to me tonight:
'Oh Acton let us be ambiguous tonight.'

Nessa

I met her on the First of August
In the Shangri-La Hotel,
She took me by the index finger
And dropped me in her well.
And that was a whirlpool, that was a whirlpool,
And I very nearly drowned.

Take off your pants, she said to me,
And I very nearly didn't;
Would you care to swim, she said to me,
And I hopped into the Irish sea.
And that was a whirlpool, that was a whirlpool,
And I very nearly drowned.

On the way back I fell in the field
And she fell down beside me.
I'd have lain in the grass with her all my life
With Nessa:
She was a whirlpool, she was a whirlpool,
And I very nearly drowned.

Oh Nessa my dear, Nessa my dear,
Will you stay with me on the rocks?
Will you come for me into the Irish sea
And for me let your red hair down?
And then we will ride into Dublin city
In a taxi-cab wrapped-up in dust.
Oh you are a whirlpool, you are a whirlpool,
And I am very nearly drowned.

Words for a Marriage

to Mark Wickham and Mary Murphy, 15 August 1974

In the days of your courtship you doubted
That a swan could nest in a place with no shelter,
On a bar of sand near a grotesque oil tanker,
And survive, and as the weeks unravelled
You kept returning to the island to make doubly certain
Until came a day she was gone –
Only naturally shattered egg shells remaining.
Now in the days of your marriage friends celebrating
Wonder how two people unusually fearless and gentle
Can marry like this, and survive, and the cliffhanging case
For your friends is that they know that you will;
Dream like a mantilla drawn back from the face
Of reality, cygnets ferried safely on her back
In flight through even ill-winds, white through black.

Tribute to a Reporter in Belfast, 1974

Poets, is not this solitary man's own uniquely
utilitarian technique of truth-telling,
this finely apparent effort of his
to split the atom of a noun and reach truth through language,
to chip-carve each word and report
as if language itself were the very conscience of reality, –
a poetry more
than poetry is?
Tonight once more he has done his work with words
and fish roots and echoes of all manner and kind
did flower up out of an ocean-floor resonance
so rapidly but with such clarity
that you were made to look out of the eyes of another
even as the other shot you dead in the back,
out of the eyes of a catholic republican
whose grandparents were quakers in Norwich,
but likewise out of the eyes
of a seventeenth-century Norfolkman in Virginia
sailing a copper knife through the soft pink air
of an Indian's open mouth. . .

Gratias for the verbal honesty of Liam Hourican
in a country where words also have died an unnatural death
or else have been used on all sides for unnatural ends
and by poets as much as by gunmen or churchmen.
Day and night his integrity of words has sustained us.

The Girl with the Keys to Pearse's Cottage

to John and Judith Meagher

When I was sixteen I met a dark girl;
Her dark hair was darker because her smile was so bright;
She was the girl with the keys to Pearse's Cottage;
And her name was Cáit Killann.

The cottage was built into the side of a hill;
I recall two windows and cosmic peace
Of bare brown rooms and on whitewashed walls
Photographs of the passionate and pale Pearse.

I recall wet thatch and peeling jambs
And how all was best seen from below in the field;
I used sit in the rushes with ledger-book and pencil
Compiling poems of passion for Cáit Killann.

Often she used linger on the sill of a window;
Hands by her side and brown legs akimbo;
In sun-red skirt and moon-black blazer;
Looking toward our strange world wide-eyed.

Our world was strange because it had no future;
She was America-bound at summer's end.
She had no choice but to leave her home –
The girl with the keys to Pearse's Cottage.

O Cáit Killann, O Cáit Killann,
You have gone with your keys from your own native place.
Yet here in this dark – El Greco eyes blaze back
From your Connemara postman's daughter's proudly mortal face.

The Day of the Starter

I have known Donal Dowd these forty years.
He may well be the biggest butcher in town
But I remember the day – and it breaks my heart
To contemplate it – when he was a messenger boy
Down in the abattoir
I may say, men, he is the same man
Today as he was forty years ago
Except of course for the casa on the hill,
His wife and six daughters.
Donal Dowd has given that woman everything – every
Conceivable gadget on this earth –
Walkie-talkie dish washer, clothes washer, carpet washer.
No, love is love: each
Morning as he starts the Rover 2000 with the automatic gears
He revs thrice for the wife.
She, beaming from the rear, shrieks after him into the exhaust:
'Oh, he's a perfect starter, he's my beau.'

The Limerickman that Went to the Bad

Well, fellas, as ye all know, I'm a Limerick stalwart
Who was chosen for the British Lions team for South Africa
And I went out there – but to play football not politics.
One night after a function in J—burg
A Limerick exile came up to me and flung his maulers around me
And naturally I thought I was amongst one of our own.
But d'ye know what he said – looking funnylike out of his
          headlights –
He said: 'I've just seen two young glorious African gentlemen
Playing handball in church.'
And with that he deliberately poured his entire pint glass of lager
Over my head.
I was not surprised to find out later that he was a spoilt priest
And that no sooner had he landed in South Africa
Than he had started co-habiting with a coloured skivvy.
Like all Limerickmen that go to the bad he had a history.
But for sheer blasphemy, can you imagine anything more fucking
          blasphemous
Than two coloureds playing handball in church? Jasus.

In the Springtime of her Life my Love Cut off her Hair

She rat-tat-tatted on the glass-paned door of our grim suburban
    home
And I unlatched it with much faith as ever and before;
But when I saw what she had done I knew pain to the myelitic bone
And saw that all I had written and worked for was no more.
For what Keats said of his long poem was true of my love's
Auburn hair – smoke in autumn but redder
Than down-goings of carrot suns on summer's eves –
'A place to wander in' in figures-of-eight along somnambulant
    rivers.
From that day on – in April cruel as ever –
A figure-of-eight was severed and I am sleepless
In a Chinese prison of all-human loneliness
In which I cannot sleep but think, think of her
As she was and – cut off from the Tree of Life – ignobly pine.
I loved her for her auburn hair and not herself alone.

The Night They Murdered Boyle Somerville

As I was travelling one morning in an empty carriage
On a train passing south through the west
A small old woman with her husband who was smaller
Hobbled in, shut the door and sat down.
They told me they were going home to Skibbereen,
That they were old age pensioners and proud of it
Enjoying free travel up and down the country.
They sat down opposite me and we conversed
When it suited us
Such was the ease with which we comported our silences.
Outside, the fields in their summer, lay on their sides in the sun,
Their season of flashing over.
Nor did we evade each other's eyes
Nor pronounce solutions to the awful war-in-progress
Except by a sign-language acknowledging
That here was the scar that lay *inside* the wound,
The self-betrayal beyond all chat.
And all this ease and all this sombre wisdom came
Not from me who am not by nature wise
But from the two old age pensioners in their seventies.
He was a king-figure from out the islands of time,
A short round-shouldered man with a globe of a skull
Whose lips were the lips of an African chieftain
Having that expression from which there is no escape,
A gaze of the lips,
Interrupted only by the ritual blowing of an ancient pipe.
His wife – being a queen – told him to put away his pipe;
Did he not see the sticker on the windowpane?
It said 'Ná Caith Tobac' – but he did not hear her
No more than he heard the ticket inspector
Who having failed to draw attention to the warning notice
Withdrew apologetically, apologising for the intrusion.
So, while the old man blew on his walnut plug
His wife gazed out the window and so did I.
When she spoke, she spoke of the old times and the *scoraíocht*

Back in Skibbereen and of the new times and the new words.
'Ah but,' he interposed, glaring out into the bluewalled sky,
'I found out what was in it, and was not in it,
The night they murdered Boyle Somerville;
I knew then that it was only the sky had a roof.'
Whereupon beads of sweat trembled on his upper lip
Between the black bristles of his pouring flesh.
Here was an old man, fit to humble death.

1972

Hymn to Nessa

Climbing back over to zero
I nearly fell over the sea
Climbing back over to zero
The sea fell over me

Behind me on the sea shore Nessa lay
She is the red sun at nightfall
Behind me on the sea shore Nessa lay
Watching me walk out to sea

I looked back and saw her wave towards me
She burned through her eyes
I looked back and saw her wave towards me
Her face burning in coals

Behind her a cliff stood with grass on it
She lay at the base of the cliff
Behind her a cliff stood with grass on it
She waved from the base of the cliff

She waved and she waved and she waved
She lay down and shuttered her eyes
She waved and she waved and she waved
Shuttering her eyes in the sun

When I looked back again she was not gone
She was sleeping under the sun
When I looked back again she was not gone
She was sleeping under the sun

Protestant Old Folks' Coach Tour of the Ring of Kerry

Although it was a summer's day
It rained as though it was winter;
And I pressed my nose against the windowpane,
The zoo-like windowpane of the coach,
And I closed my eyes and dreamed,
Dreamed that I was swimming,
Swimming in the coves of Kerry
With my young man Danny
And no one else about;
Danny, Danny, dripping wet,
Laughing through his teeth;
Blown to bits at Ypres.
Behind my eyes it is sunshine still
Although he has gone;
And my mother and father pad about the farm
Like ghosts cut out of cardboard;
When they died I too looked ghostly
But I stayed alive although I don't know how;
Dreaming to put the beehives back on their feet,
Waiting for Danny to come home.
And now I'm keeping house for brother Giles
Who stayed at home today to milk the cows;
Myself, I am a great jowled cow untended
And when I die I would like to die alone.

The Difficulty that is Marriage

We disagree to disagree, we divide, we differ;
Yet each night as I lie in bed beside you
And you are faraway curled up in sleep
I array the moonlit ceiling with a mosaic of question-marks;
How was it I was so lucky to have ever met you?
I am no brave pagan proud of my mortality,
Yet gladly on this changeling earth I should live for ever
If it were with you, my sleeping friend.
I have my troubles and I shall always have them
But I should rather live with you for ever
Than exchange my troubles for a changeless kingdom.
But I do not put you on a pedestal or throne;
You must have your faults but I do not see them.
If it were with you, I should live for ever.

Lord Mayo

I had to go and work in office-blocks in Shepherd's Bush
    And I worked such hours that I could not write letters;
I spent my few free hours in The Railway Tavern talking
    With a Carlow-born clerk and two Belfast bricklayers;
But I came back to you, Lord Mayo.

Now you are older and angrier and I am still young and gay
    And what, my lord, are we going to do?
If you were but to smile once as once you used to
    I'd jump into bed with you for ever;
For I came back to you, Lord Mayo.

I'd go live with you in the wilds of Erris
    Rearing children despite bog and rain;
I'd row with you the dark depths of Beltra and of Conn
    If you'd but smile on me;
For I came back to you, Lord Mayo.

The Hat Factory

Eleven o'clock and the bar is empty
Except for myself and an old man;
We sit with our backs to the street-window,
The sun in the east streaming through it;
And I think of childhood and swimming
Underwater by a famine pier;
The ashlar coursing of the stonework
Like the bar-room shelves
Seen through tidal amber seaweed
In the antique mirror;
Now myself and the old man floating
In the glow of the early morning sun
Twined round each other and our newspapers;
And our pint glasses like capstans on the pier.
We do not read our daily charters
— Charters of liberty to know what's going on —
But hold them as capes before reality's bull
And with grace of ease we make our passes;
El Cordobes might envy this old small man
For the sweet veronicas he makes in daily life.
He is the recipient of an old age pension
While I am so low in society's scale
I do not rate even the dole
But I am at peace with myself and so is he;
Although I do not know what he is thinking
His small round fragile noble mouth
Has the look of the door of Aladdin's cave
Quivering in expectation of the magic word;
Open sesame;
I suspect that like me he is thinking
Of the nothing-in-particular;
Myself, I am thinking of the local hat factory,
Of its history and the eerie fact
That in my small town I have never known
Anyone who worked in it
Or had to do with it at all;

As a child I used look through a hole in the hedge
At the hat factory down below in the valley;
I used lie flat on my face in the long grass
And put out my head through the hole;
Had the hatters looked out through their porthole windows
They would have seen high up in the hillside
A long wild hedgerow broken only
By the head of the child looking out through the hole;
I speculate;
And as to what kind of hats they make;
And do they have a range in black birettas;
And do they have a conveyor belt of toppers;
And do the workers get free hats?
And I recall the pope's skull-cap
Placed on my head when as a boy-child
In a city hospital I lay near to death
And the black homburg of the red-nosed undertaker
And the balaclavas of assassins
And the pixies of the lost children of the murdered earth;
And the multi-coloured yamulka of the wandering Jew
And the black kippa of my American friend
In Jerusalem in the snow
And the portly Egyptian's tiny fez
And the tragic Bedouin's kefia in the sands of sun
And the monk's cowl and the nun's wimple
And the funereal mortarboards of airborn puritans
And the megalithic coifs of the pan-cake women of Brittany
And the sleek fedoras of well-to-do thugs
And sadistic squires' napoleonic tricorns
And prancing horse-cavalry in their cruel shakos
And the heroic lifeboatman's black sou'wester
And the nicotine-stained wig of the curly-haired barrister
And the black busby used as a handbag by my laughing
        brother
And the silken turban of the highbrow widow
And foreign legionaries in nullah kepis
And Mayday praesidiums in astrakhans
And bonnets and boaters and sombreros and stetsons
And stove-pipes and steeples and mantillas and berets

And topis and sun-hats and deer-stalkers and pill-boxes
And naughty grandmothers in toques
And bishops' mitres and soldier's helmets;
And in Languedoc and in Aran – cloth caps.
And what if you were a hatter
And you married a hatter
And all your sons and daughters worked as hatters
And you inhabited a hat-house all full of hats:
Hats, hats, hats, hats:
Hats: the apotheosis of an ancient craft
And I think of all the nationalities of Israel
And of how each always clings to his native hat,
His priceless and moveable roof,
His hat which is the last and first symbol
Of a man's slender foothold on this earth.
Women and girls also work in the factory
But not many of them wear hats;
Some wear scarves, but rarely hats;
Now there'll be no more courting of maidens
In schooner hats on dangerous cliffs;
It seems part of the slavery of liberation
To empty relationships of all courtship
Of which hats were an exciting part.
Probably, I shall never wear a hat:
So thus I ask the old man
If I may look at his trilby
– Old honesty –
And graciously he hands it to me
And with surprise
I note that it was manufactured
In the local hat factory
And I hand it back to him
– A crown to its king –
And like a king he blesses me when he goes
Wishing me a good day before he starts
His frail progress home along the streets,
Along the lanes and terraces of the hillside,
To his one up and one down.
I turn about and see

Over the windowpane's frosted hemisphere
A small black hat sail slowly past my eyes
Into the unknown ocean of the sun at noon.

Wife Who Smashed Television Gets Jail

'She came home, my Lord, and smashed-in the television;
Me and the kids were peaceably watching Kojak
When she marched into the living-room and declared
That if I didn't turn off the television immediately
She'd put her boot through the screen;
I didn't turn it off, so instead she turned it off
— I remember the moment exactly because Kojak
After shooting a dame with the same name as my wife
Snarled at the corpse — Goodnight, Queen Maeve —
And then she took off her boots and smashed-in the television;
I had to bring the kids round to my mother's place;
We got there just before the finish of Kojak;
(My mother has a fondness for Kojak, my Lord);
When I returned home my wife had deposited
What was left of the television into the dustbin,
Saying — I didn't get married to a television
And I don't see why my kids or anybody else's kids
Should have a television for a father or mother,
We'd be much better off all down in the pub talking
Or playing bar-billiards —
Whereupon she disappeared off back down again to the pub.'
Justice O'Brádaigh said wives who preferred bar-billiards to family
          television
Were a threat to the family which was the basic unit of society
As indeed the television itself could be said to be a basic unit of the
          family
And when as in this case wives expressed their preference in forms of
          violence
Jail was the only place for them. Leave to appeal was refused.

Polycarp

Polycarp has quit the priesthood
And he is living back at home;
He wears a smile upon his lips
That blooms from the marrow bone.

It's a smile that flowers and withers
Like fruit upon a tree;
In winter he stands at corners
In the streets all nakedly.

And they are waxing pretty angry —
Are Respectability's crew;
It's a crime against all decency
To be one of the very few

Who has had courage like Polycarp
To be his own sweet self;
Not to mind the small town sneers
When they call him a 'fucking elf'

Or the do-it-yourself-men boors
Who detest men with feminine souls;
Boors who when they were boys
Spoke of women as 'ruddy holes'

And now who are married and proper
Living up on Respectability Hill
And in their spare time make their own coffins
Which they use first as coffee tables.

But Polycarp polkas the streets
As free and easy as he feels;
Sometimes he walks on his toes,
Sometimes on his heels.

Yet they'll put him upon his knees
In the amphitheatre soon;
But his smile will wear them down
By the blood-light of the moon;

And in summer's golden rains
He'll burst out in fruit all over;
She's here, she's here, she's here;
And it is Polycarp that knows how to love her.

Swags of red apples are his cheeks;
Swags of yellow pears are his eyes;
Foliages of dark green oaks are his torsos;
And in the cambium of his bark juice lies.

Desire under the steeples and spires,
Polycarp's back in town;
Desire under the steeples and spires,
Polycarp's back in town.

Anna Swanton

I met her on the road to Ballavarry;
She asked me why do boys always hurry;
When I told her I had the Dublin train to take
She turned and said she'd come and wave goodbye.

Along that wide road blue green and dusty
That lopes along the land to Ballavarry
I listened to her words come over to me
As from over the most deserted ancient valley.

We walked along the platform at Ballavarry;
I stopped to pluck daisies to make a chain;
I put it round her neck and although it parted
I did not make another for we have not.

For the train no more stopped at Ballavarry;
It had stopped for the last time the week before;
Next year we got the stationmaster's cottage
And our children are growing up playing real trains.

And yet although I live in terror of the tracks
For fear that they should prove our children's grave
I live in greater terror of the thought
Of life without Anna Swanton on this earth:

Or of how I might be rich in far-off Nottingham
And married to another kind of girl;
I'd rather rain for ever in the fields with Anna Swanton
Than a car or a goddess in the sun.

Three Hundred Men Made Redundant

It is shocking, Hilda, shocking;
300 men made redundant;
I have to collect a sirloin at the butcher's;
I'll see you at the hairdresser's in half-an-hour.

300 men made redundant;
Indeed, indeed, how shocking, how shocking;
I forgot to tell Madge about the card-game for Sunday;
If I see her at the hairdresser's I'll tell her then.

Good day, Fr Ryan, I'm very well, how are you?
Thanks be to God and His Holy Mother;
300 men made redundant;
Perfectly shocking, perfectly shocking.

Kindly, Fr Ryan, give the pulpit a clean-up;
I find the handrail has become a bit sticky;
Which reminds me I must make a note of it;
300 men made redundant.

But we have bigger issues to thrash out
Than 300 men made redundant;
For example the evils of family planning –
Not to mention mixed marriages and mixed education.

(Sing) 300 men made redundant
300 men made redundant
300 men made redundant
– And the evils of family planning.

She Mends an Ancient Wireless

You never claimed to be someone special;
Sometimes you said you had no special talent;
Yet I have seen you rear two dancing daughters
With care and patience and love unstinted;
Reading or telling stories, knitting gansies
And all the while holding down a job
In the teeming city, morning until dusk.
And in the house when anything went wrong
You were the one who fixed it without fuss;
The electricity switch which was neither on nor off,
The tv aerial forever falling out;
And now as I watch you mend an ancient wireless
From my tiny perch I cry once more your praises
And call out your name across the great divide – Nessa.

Trauma Junction

The answer to your question is that I am not your mother;
Your mother was another mother and she died in Russia.

Him

His name was Christmas and he was a refugee;
And he moved through his exile like waves through a landless sea.

Bugs Bunny

There is a schoolteacher in my town and he looks like Bugs Bunny;
He is a mass murderer and I am not being funny.

Teresa's Bar

We sat all day in Teresa's Bar
And talked, or did not talk, the time away;
The only danger was that we might not leave sober
But that is a price you have to pay.
Outside in the rain the powers-that-be
Chemist, draper, garda, and priest
Paced up and down in unspeakable rage
That we could sit all day in Teresa's Bar
'Doing nothing'.

Behind the bar it was often empty;
Teresa, like all of us,
Besides doing nothing
Had other things to do
Such as cooking meals
Or washing out underwear
For her mad father
And her madder husband,
Or enduring their screams.

But Teresa deep down had no time for time
Or for those whose business has to do with time;
She would lean against the bar and smile through her weariness
By turns being serious and light with us;
Her eyes like birds on the waves of the sea;
A mother-figure but also a sun-girl;
An image of tranquillity but of perpetual creation;
A process in which there is no contradiction
For those with guts not to be blackmailed by time.

There is no time in Teresa's Bar;
The Garda Síochána or the Guardia Civil –
The Junior Chamber or the Roman Curia –
The Poetry Society or the GAA –
The Rugby Club or the Maynooth Hierarchy –
RTE or Conor's Cabaret –

It makes no difference in Teresa's Bar
Where the air is as annotated with the tobacco smoke of
         inventiveness
As the mind of a Berkleyan philosopher.

The small town abounds with rumours
About Teresa's Bar;
A hive of drug-takers (poor bees)
A nest of fornicators (poor birds)
Homosexual not to mention heterosexual;
Poor birds and bees trapped in metaphors of malice.
The truth is that here as along by the path
By the river that flows along by the edge of the town
Young and old meet in a life-obtaining sequence
Of days interspersed by nights, seasons by seasons,
Deaths by deaths;
While the members of the resurrection of judgement
Growl and scowl behind arrases in drawing-rooms
Here are the members of the resurrection of life
And their tutelary goddess is Teresa
Thirty-five, small, heavy, and dark,
And who would sleep with any man who was honest enough
Not to mouth the platitudes of love;
A sensual woman, brave and true,
Bringer of dry wisdom and free laughter
As well as of glasses and bowls,
And who has sent forth into the hostile world
Persons whose universal compassion is infinitesimally more catholic
Than that of any scion of academe
Such as James Felix Hennessy
Who has been on the dole for sixteen years
As well as making poems and reading books
And who when accused of obscenity
By the Right Rev. Fr O'Doherty
Riposted with all the humility of Melchisedech:
'You must learn the reality of the flesh, Father;
You must learn the reality of the flesh.'

If there be a heaven
Heaven would be
Being with Teresa
Inside the rain;
So let's lock up the bar Teresa,
Lay ourselves on the floor,
Put some more coal on the fire,
Pour ourselves each a large whiskey; .
Let's drink to Teresa of Teresa's Bar
Reclining on the floor with one of her boys,
And big black coals burning bright,
And yellowest whiskey in a brown bottle,
And outside a downpour relentlessly pouring down.

The Baker

After a night at the ovens
In the big city bakery
The baker walks home alone:
He stalks through the dawn
Gropingly
Like a man through a plate-glass door
(There have been many such –
Oh many such – years
And nights of it
And it has been so
Hot)
He feels fragile and eerily pure
Like a loaf new out of oven,
All heat through-and-through,
And he does not look sure
That the air is not a plate-glass door;
So gropingly he stalks
In his hob-nailed boots
Up the steep terraced street:
Like a tiny giant walking in glue:
Like a human being about to split in two.

Two in a Boat

She took one oar and I took the other
But mine had slipped from me when she pulled on hers;
And then when at last I had got a grip
She had raised hers in victory glittering over sable waters,
The sun merely accentuating victory's glitter in each pearly globule.
And so we pulled in opposite directions,
Drifting out of quarrels into accidents and out of accidents into
        quarrels.
I thought of our two children in another country and of their being
        free
From their parents until came a collision
With two other frail craft and later
Drifting onto a grass bank we had to be pushed out into the sun
        again.
But the sun did not alter the pattern until out of the blue
Came glorious fresh rain
And pulling in opposite directions we reached land again.

The Weeping Headstones of the Isaac Becketts

The Protestant graveyard was a forbidden place
So naturally as children we explored its precincts:
Clambered over drystone walls under elms and chestnuts,
Parted long grasses and weeds, poked about under yews,
Reconnoitred the chapel whose oak doors were always closed,
Stared at the schist headstones of the Isaac Becketts.
And then we would depart with mortal sins in our bones
As ineradicable as an arthritis;
But we had seen enough to know what the old folks meant
When we would overhear them whisperingly at night refer to
'The headstones of the Becketts – they would make you weep'.
These arthritises of sin:
But although we had only six years each on our backs
We could decipher
Brand-new roads open up through heaven's fields
And upon them – like thousands upon thousands
Of pilgrims kneeling in the desert –
The weeping headstones of the Isaac Becketts.

In Memory of Those Murdered in the Dublin Massacre, May 1974

In the grime-ridden sunlight in the downtown Wimpy bar
I think of all the crucial aeons – and of the labels
That freedom fighters stick onto the lost destinies of unborn
      children;
The early morning sunlight carries in the whole street from outside;
The whole wide street from outside through the plate-glass
      windows;
Wholly, sparklingly, surgingly, carried in from outside;
And the waitresses cannot help but be happy and gay
As they swipe at the table-tops with their dishcloths –
Such a moment as would provide the heroic freedom fighter
With his perfect meat.
And I think of those heroes – heroes? – and how truly
Obscene is war.

And as I stand up to walk out –
The aproned old woman who's been sweeping the floor
Has mop stuck in bucket, leaning on it;
And she's trembling all over, like a flower in the breeze.
She'd make a mighty fine explosion now, if you were to blow her up;
An explosion of petals, of aeons, and the waitresses too, flying
      breasts and limbs,
For a free Ireland.

Maud Gonne MacBride's Mayo

Over at where the stream went under the ground
Under the orchard wall
A dog, a black-and-white terrier, yelped at the vanishing water.

I saw the chaperones and the girls
As though they had been born but should never die;
The chaperones who had turned away
From the cool white core of the wood
To lean on tip-toe on the cliff-edge of the meadow;
And at the cool white core
Under the low strung streaming branches of the oak
Sleeping girls lay floating on their backs
Above the winding grass;
Increase of light did not shut their eyes
Nor the old horse that later staggered past
As though by accident;
Past the well full of floating leaves
And the teacups that were filling with clay.

And the big house loomed as though either empty or not.

The clouds – doves from Africa – marked time in the hill:
Then it came:
In spite of their nakedness – such sea floor and such waves –
The sleeping girls burst into rain
As though they were the fire inside the rain;
And their faces were flashed onto the windowpanes
Of all trains leaving Paris for the East
And they went out over the same stile,
        The same fall,
Like raindrops off the peak of a boy king's cap.

In some twigs stood a vast cathedral roofless,
Its forests of red spires yearning for her milky breast.

Before the Celtic Yoke

What was it like in Ireland before the Celtic yoke –
Before war insinuated its slime into the forests of the folk?

Elizabethan, Norman, Viking, Celt,
Conquistadores all:
Imperialists, racialists, from across the seas,
Merciless whalesback riders
Thrusting their languages down my virgin throat,
And to rape not merely but to garotte
My human voice:
To screw my soul to orthodoxy and break my neck.

But I survive, recall
That these are but Micky-come-latelies
Puritanical, totalitarian, by contrast with my primal tongue:
My vocabularies are boulders cast up on time's beaches;
Masses of sea-rolled stones reared up in mile-high ricks
Along the shores and curving coasts of all my island;
Verbs dripping fresh from geologic epochs;
Scorched, drenched, in metamorphosis, vulcanicity, ice ages.

No Celt
Nor Viking, Norman, Elizabethan,
Could exterminate me –
I am as palpable and inscrutable
As is a mother to her man-child;
If you would contemplate me
You will know the terror that an old man knows
As he shrinks back from the grassy womb of his chirping mamma.

In Ireland before the Celtic yoke I was the voice of Seeing
And my island people's Speaking was their Being;
So go now brother – cast off all cultural shrouds
And speak like me – like the mighty sun through the clouds.

The Archbishop Dreams of the Harlot of Rathkeale

My dream is non-committal – it is no sin –
(Thomas, I think, would be tickled by it –
As indeed I am myself; in it is a neat point)
I am simply lying here in my double-bed
Dreaming of the harlot of Rathkeale;
I see her walking down the road at evening
Wearing a red scarf and black high-heel shoes;
She is wearing nothing else and the sun
In the western sky is a-dying slowly
In a blue sky half as old as time;
A car approaches her but from behind
Resembling palely an approaching elephant
Seen through binoculars in the bush;
It does not halt – I think the driver
Is too shocked – he looks back aghast –
A god-fearing man – and in my dream, I laugh
And say her name out aloud in my mind
'Esmé – Esmé, the harlot of Rathkeale';
She is walking towards me when the dream ends
And I wake up in the morning feeling like an old bull
Plumb to charge through my brethren in my sermon.

The Kilfenora Teaboy

I'm the Kilfenora teaboy
And I'm not so very young,
But though the land is going to pieces
I will not take up the gun;
I am happy making tea,
I make lots of it when I can,
And when I can't – I just make do;
And I do a small bit of sheepfarming on the side.

Oh but it's the small bit of furze between two towns
Is what makes the Kilfenora teaboy really run.

I have nine healthy daughters
And please God I will have more,
Sometimes my dear wife beats me
But on the whole she's a gentle soul;
When I'm not making her some tea
I sit out and watch them all
Ring-a-rosying in the street;
And I do a small bit of sheepfarming on the side.

Oh but it's the small bit of furze between two towns
Is what makes the Kilfenora teaboy really run.

Oh indeed my wife is handsome,
She has a fire lighting in each eye,
You can pluck laughter from her elbows
And from her knees pour money's tears;
I make all my tea for her,
I'm her teaboy on the hill,
And I also thatch her roof;
And I do a small bit of sheepfarming on the side.

Oh but it's the small bit of furze between two towns
Is what makes the Kilfenora teaboy really run.

And I'm not only a famous teaboy,
I'm a famous caveman too;
I paint pictures by the hundred
But you can't sell walls;
Although the people praise my pictures
As well as my turf-perfumed blend
They rarely fling a fiver in my face;
Oh don't we do an awful lot of dying on the side?

But Oh it's the small bit of furze between two towns
Is what makes the Kilfenora teaboy really run.

What is a Protestant, Daddy?

Gaiters were sinister
And you dared not
Glance up at the visage;
It was a long lean visage
With a crooked nose
And beaked dry lips
And streaky gray hair
And they used scurry about
In small black cars
(Unlike Catholic bishops
Stately in big cars
Or Pope Pius XII
In his gold-plated Cadillac)
And they'd make dashes for it
Across deserted streets
And disappear quickly
Into vast cathedrals
All silent and aloof,
Forlorn and leafless,
Their belfry louvres
Like dead men's lips,
And whose congregations, if any,
Were all octogenarian
With names like Iris;
More likely
There were no congregations
And these rodent-like clergymen
Were conspirators;
You could see it in their faces;
But as to what the conspiracies
Were about, as children
We were at a loss to know;
Our parents called them 'parsons'
Which turned them from being rodents
Into black hooded crows
Evilly flapping their wings

About our virginal souls;
And these 'parsons' had wives –
As unimaginable a state of affairs
As it would have been to imagine
A pope in a urinal;
Protestants were Martians
Light-years more weird
Than zoological creatures;
But soon they would all go away
For as a species they were dying out,
Soon there would be no more Protestants. . .
O Yea, O Lord,
I was a proper little Irish Catholic boy
Way back in the 1950s.

Parents

A child's face is a drowned face:
Her parents stare down at her asleep
Estranged from her by a sea:
She is under the sea
And they are above the sea:
If she looked up she would see them
As if locked out of their own home,
Their mouths open
And their foreheads furrowed:
Pursed-up orifices of fearful fish
And their big ears like fins behind glass:
And in her sleep she is calling out to them
      Father, Father
      Mother, Mother
But they cannot hear her:
She is inside the sea
And they are outside the sea:
And, through the night, stranded, they stare
At the drowned, drowned face of their child.

Going Home to Mayo, Winter, 1949

Leaving behind us the alien, foreign city of Dublin
My father drove through the night in an old Ford Anglia,
His five-year-old son in the seat beside him,
The rexine seat of red leatherette,
And a yellow moon peered in through the windscreen.
'Daddy, Daddy,' I cried, 'Pass out the moon,'
But no matter how hard he drove he could not pass out the moon.
Each town we passed through was another milestone
And their names were magic passwords into eternity:
Kilcock, Kinnegad, Strokestown, Elphin,
Tarmonbarry, Tulsk, Ballaghaderreen, Ballavarry;
Now we were in Mayo and the next stop was Turlough,
The village of Turlough in the heartland of Mayo,
And my father's mother's house, all oil-lamps and women,
And my bedroom over the public bar below,
And in the morning cattle-cries and cock-crows:
Life's seemingly seamless garment gorgeously rent
By their screeches and bellowings. And in the evenings
I walked with my father in the high grass down by the river
Talking with him – an unheard-of thing in the city.

But home was not home and the moon could be no more outflanked
Than the daylight nightmare of Dublin city:
Back down along the canal we chugged into the city
And each lock-gate tolled our mutual doom;
And railings and palings and asphalt and traffic-lights,
And blocks after blocks of so-called 'new' tenements –
Thousands of crosses of loneliness planted
In the narrowing grave of the life of the father;
In the wide, wide cemetery of the boy's childhood.

Fat Molly

I was fostered out to a woman called Fat Molly:
It was in the year 744
On the other side of the forest from the monk-fort at Kells
Where the bird-men were scribing their magnificent comic
The Book of Kells.
I'd say Molly was about thirty when I went to her
And she taught me the art of passionate kissing:
From minuscule kisses to majuscule
On lips, breasts, neck, shoulders, and lips,
And the enwrapping of tongue around tongue;
I was about fourteen
And she used make me kiss her for hours non-stop
And I'd sit in her lap with my hands
Around her waist gulping her down
And eating her green apples
That hung in bunches from her thighs
And the clusters of hot grapes between her breasts
Until from the backs of my ears down to my toes
All of me tingled
And in the backs of her eyes I saw that her glass had no bottom;
Nothing in life afterwards ever tasted quite so luscious
As Fat Molly's kisses;
              O spirals of animals,
Interlaces of birds;
Sweet, warm, and wet, were the kisses she kissed;
Juicy oranges on a naked platter.
She lived all alone in a crannóg
Which had an underwater zig-zag causeway
And people said – and it was not altogether a fiction –
That only a completely drunk man
Could successfully negotiate Fat Molly's entrance;
Completely drunk, I used stagger home
And fall asleep in the arms of her laughter:
O sweet crucifixion, crucified on each other.

Well, that was half-a-century ago

And now the Vikings are here –
Bloody foreigners –
And there's nothing but blood in the air:
But thank you Fat Molly for a grand education;
Like all great education it was perfectly useless.

Poetry, a Natural Thing

Basking salmon under the salmon bridge at Galway
or: a deer at a window-sill of Magdalen College
being fed bread-crumbs by my friend Michael Lurgan –
It was October and he was reading Proust
and I was an inmate of a London hostel for homeless boys

Where I shared a room with a boy from Blackpool
whose silence was the silence of a bear in a cave
and who had a passion for looking at himself in the looking-glass:
I had the feeling that he had the makings of a policeman
and that one day he would truncheon somebody to death.

But basking salmon of self-sufficiency or, supplicant deer,
or, answers to questions, always remain:
It is not I who am hiding in the trees from my father:
it is he who is hiding in the trees, and he is waiting to ambush me
as I step out the bright forest path to the spring.

That's poetry, a natural thing.

Marguerite

Three years after you left convent school
You were still a convent girl, Marguerite:
Your appleblossom cheeks, your bronze curls,
And your eyes – your forever looking-upwards eyes
In the huge depths of whose innocence swam
Male fish as predatory as piranhas.

Years later still you had not changed
Although the scene and circumstances had:
Oh, they radically had. 'I have a child'
You said, as we stood in the middle of London,
Two exiles outside the entrance to the Tube:
I realised that you lived alone with your child.

'I have a flat on the Balham side of Clapham Common'
You said so eagerly – as if nothing had changed:
Now your innocence hurt because I could not accept
That a girl like you should so cheerfully endure
Such solitary exile in that foreign megalatropolis
For being an unmarried mother in Dublin, 4.

Oh, where are you, tonight, Marguerite?
Last night I had a dream that you had drowned
Your child in the bath and hung yourself
In the lavatory of your Clapham flat:
Now day is vanishing down the chute of dusk:
Oh, where are you, tonight, Marguerite?

Backside to the Wind

A fourteen-year-old boy is out rambling alone
By the scimitar shores of Killala Bay
And he is dreaming of a French Ireland,
Backside to the wind.

What kind of village would I now be living in?
French vocabularies intertwined with Gaelic
And Irish women with French fathers,
Backsides to the wind.

The Ballina Road would become the Rue de Humbert
And wine would be the staple drink of the people;
A staple diet of potatoes and wine,
Backsides to the wind.

Monsieur O'Duffy might be the harbour-master
And Madame Duffy the mother of thirteen
Tiny philosophers to overthrow Maynooth,
Backsides to the wind.

Father Molloy might be a worker-priest
Up to his knees in manure at the cattle-mart;
And dancing and loving on the streets at evening
Backsides to the wind.

Jean Arthur Rimbaud might have grown up here
In a hillside terrace under the round tower;
Would he, like me, have dreamed of an Arabian Dublin,
Backside to the wind?

Garda Ned MacHale might now be a gendarme
Having hysterics at the crossroads;
Excommunicating male motorists, ogling females,
Backside to the wind.

I walk on, facing the village ahead of me,
A small concrete oasis in the wild countryside;
Not the embodiment of the dream of a boy,
Backside to the wind.

Seagulls and crows, priests and nuns,
Perch on the rooftops and steeples,
And their Anglo-American mores asphyxiate me,
Backside to the wind.

Not to mention the Japanese invasion:
Blunt people as serious as ourselves
And as humourless; money is our God,
Backsides to the wind.

The medieval Franciscan Friary of Moyne
Stands house-high, roofless, by;
Past it rolls a vast asphalt pipe,
Backside to the wind,

Ferrying chemical waste out to sea
From the Asahi synthetic-fibre plant;
Where once monks sang, wage-earners slave,
Backsides to the wind.

Run on, sweet River Moy,
Although I end my song; you are
The scales of a salmon of a boy,
Backside to the wind.

Yet I have no choice but to leave, to leave,
And yet there is nowhere I more yearn to live
Than in my own wild countryside,
Backside to the wind.

1976

The Death of Constance Purfield

When Constance Purfield was in her eighty-fourth year
She requested me to drive her out to a country graveyard
Thirteen miles outside Dublin: it was Autumn
And in her shrill, biscuit-tin voice
She waxed grandiloquent on the new estates,
Chirping: 'But I prefer the trees.'

At the graveyard everything was prepared
(She had made all the arrangements herself –
A singular, single lady to the last)
And, the suave surgeon with the toothbrush moustache
Having injected her,
And the small priest having stuttered Last Prayers
While she, like a conductor, conducted him
She wished me well in the war-riven world
And tweaking the surgeon on the cheek
She chuckled
'I eat surgeon for breakfast, you know'
And bidding me Adieu
(She reminded me of a Wild Goose Earl
Climbing into a currach at nightfall
In a hidden cove on the western coast)
She clambered into the coffin
Which was immediately lidded
And by four ropes
Lowered down into the deep grave:
Speedily the gravediggers filled it in,
Their spades plashing like oars,
And as I drove back into the Hole of Light
– Into the City of Dublin –
I could hear her shrill, biscuit-tin voice come over the seas
Chirping: 'But I prefer the trees.'

Gogo's Late Wife Tranquilla

Snapshots of my late wife Tranquilla
From albums she will never see again
— Thin but she was always thin
— Thin on the ground
— And spectacles made her look even thinner
— And long thin dresses and big floppy hats
— Only last week she thought she was thinner
— Fifty years, we were wed, fifty years
— And this week she's my late wife Tranquilla
— But last week she was my missus Mrs Gogo.

Sam's Cross

I can see Kitty waiting for me at the end of the long boreen:
I am about to drop dead but she is serene.

Sunday's Well
for Anna and Erik

A harpsichord does not build itself:
A family is a harpsichord.

Nora and Hilda

When Nora O'Mahony's widowed mother died
A stranger moved into the long house to live with her:
She was young and quiet and pretty and gay
And her name was Hilda O'Carroll.

Now the village in winter was no pretty, gay place:
Either rain or sea-wind was forever pouring:
And the skies were streets where all the shop-windows were broken
And people's faces were broken glass.

But although it was winter Hilda moved through the rough
Year like the girl in the ballad through the fair:
She was forever hastening to her own wedding:
For she was deeply in love with Nora O'Mahony.

And Nora was old and wild and angry and sad
And her long gray clothes matched her long gray hair
And she had no time for religion and politics:
All the people of the village detested her.

They had always detested her but when Hilda arrived
Their detestation blossomed into a murderous envy:
As they watched Hilda waltz out to do the messages
The women's eyes were as lecherous as the men's.

When April arrived Hilda opened a boutique
In what formerly was the living-room of the O'Mahony house:
In the window where once a sacred heart lamp had glowed
Transparent yellow dresses lay draped on olive green sofas.

The villagers snarled that Nora O'Mahony's father
Would have revolved in his grave at this obscene sacrilege:
But they were wrong for the father had loved his daughter
And had taught her that Christ lived not in lamps and statues

But occasionally in human hearts made of flesh and blood.
In summer the sea was barren of salmon
But the boutique was thronged with visitors from afar:
Not from the metropoli of the USA

But from the towns and villages of the hinterland.
And Hilda sold them her dresses like bunches of wild flowers
While Nora reposed in the back-room with books and whiskey;
And in the evenings Hilda knelt at her feet

While Nora read *Lycidas* and *Memorabilia*.
It was all compline by the fireside at evening
After the divine but painful office of the human day
And when at last the orange sun slipped softly

Off the mantelpiece of the world, they also slipped
Softly into one another's arms and in the red glow
Each dreamed the other was a boy
And in the white morning they rose white-faced with the sun

Until October and the daybreak of another year
Of door-slamming and soul-shattering:
Whether or not they will commit suicide
Is, unlike the village they live in, an open question.

Two History Professors Found Guilty of Murder

This morning in the Central Criminal Court in Dublin
Two Professors of History at the University of Mullingar,
Columba A. Cantwell and Columba B. Cantwell,
Were found guilty of the murder of Jesus Trinidad,
A thirty-year-old West Indian tutor in history at Mullingar.

Justice Columba C. Cantwell sentenced both accused to life
      imprisonment
Suspended on condition that they never get caught again.
The jury, who took a record thirty seconds to reach their verdict,
Were recommended for full-time jury service.

Earlier, evidence had been given by Mrs Jesus Trinidad
That the two professors had called to her mud-hut
In the backwoods of Mullingar
On the night of the 12th of July with a carpet-bag
Which they handed to her: it contained
Chopped-up segments of her husband's head.
However, she continued, this had come as no surprise
As for the last three years her husband had come home each day
      crying
'They are using a bacon-slicer on my mind — I cannot survive.'

After having handed over the carpet-bag to her
The two professors had said: Apart from the fact that your husband
Was a disgustingly intelligent West Indian, a Witty Wog,
He had consistently encouraged his students to ascertain the true
      facts
Of the history of Ulster, despite constant warnings not to do so.
Finally, the two professors had themselves attended Trinidad's
      tutorials
In the hope of brow-beating him: as a last resort
They took it in turns to excrete on the floor throughout his tutorials
But not even this esoteric ploy changed Trinidad's attitude:
Therefore, they said, they had no choice but to apply a final solution.

Justice Cantwell said that Trinidad was both a foreigner and a fool
And no tears whatsoever should be shed on behalf of his wife.
The court expressed sympathy with the two murderers
And wished them continued, further success in the green fields
– In the green, green, green fields – of their academic endeavours.

1978

Memoirs of a Fallen Blackbird

They liked me when I was on the wing
And I could whistle and I could sing;
But now that I am in my bed of clay
They come no more for to be with me.

It was on the main road half-way between
Newcastle West and Abbeyfeale;
A juggernaut glanced me as it passed me by
And that was the end of the road for me.

Later that day, as I lay on the verge,
A thin rake of a young man picked me up
Into his trembling hands, and he stared
At me full quarter of an hour, he stared

At me and then he laid me down
And with his hands scooped me a shallow grave;
His soul passed into me as he covered me o'er;
I fear for him now where'er he be.

They liked me when I was on the wing
And I could whistle and I could sing;
But now that I am in my bed of clay
They come no more for to be with me.

The Married Man who Fell in Love with a Semi-State Body

Ted Rice was that abnormal creature – a normal man:
Merrily married, he was a good husband to his wife,
A good father to his children, and a friendly neighbour:
Until in the winter of 1964 he resigned his job
As manager of a centre-city pub to become
An executive with a Semi-State Body, Bord Ól,
In charge of the promotion of the Alcohol Industry.
So much did Ted Rice grow to love the Semi-State Body,
So hard he worked for her,
So heroically he hullaballoo'd for her,
So hopefully he hopped for her,
So heartily he hooted for her,
So hoity-toitily he hocked for her,
So harshly he harped for her,
So headlong he hunted for her,
That he began to think of her as The Woman in his Life
And one day as the train shot slowly down the line towards Cork
He had a vision of her as an American negress in a state of semi-
    undress
And, as such, he introduced her to the Cork Chamber of Commerce:
Even the most drunken members of his audience blinked
As Mr Rice introduced the invisible woman standing beside him;
And when, in the peroration of his speech, he fondled her breasts
Temperance men broke their pledges and ordered double-brandies:
When Mr Rice departed for the railway station on the arm of his
    queen
He left behind him the Metropole Hotel strewn with bodies;
And half-way up the line he pulled the excommunication cord
And, introducing his Semi-State Body to the medieval ruins of a
    friary, declared:
'Let us sleep here together until the advertising boys arrive. . .'
Since then he has eked out the years in a mental hospital ward,
Tramping up and down the aisle of gloom in a shower of tears,
Repeating over and over: 'I loved her, I loved her.'

The Butterfly Collector of Corofin

The Butterfly Collector of Corofin
Is himself a butterfly: in a red cardigan
And skintight pants striped bluegreen
And white cravat stippled with yellow
He flutters about the back-garden
Completely at home amongst the 'speckled woods' and the 'red
    admirals':
A thirty-five-year-old male creature of shyness.
And he flutters about in the living-room also
Crying out: 'Would you?' or 'Shall I?' or 'Oh dear, no'
And should a female enter into the room
He hovers about her before swooping downstairs
Out into the flowery street of the village.
Spinning, he spins into a pub
Whose darkness yields him respite
And after a few pints and a couple of large whiskeys
He confides to the squirrel of a boy-barman:
'If only I could go back to being a caterpillar again
But there is no going back:
No going back for an old butterfly like me;
My life is a process of being crushed gradually to death.
Then, I will be collected by the Great Collector Himself:
He, the Invisible One, in the Country of the Long Grass
Casting wide his vast sieve-mesh net.
But what then? Does he put us all under glass
For ever – for the benefit of the keen-eyed arch-angels
Labelling us by our names and addresses:
E.g. Eamonn de Valera, Áras an Uactaráin,
Or Molly Malone, The Coombe, Dublin?
No, the idea does not bear thinking about:
To be transfixed for ever in a cruel unrest.
I want only to be a caterpillar again'
Cries out the Butterfly Collector of Corofin:
But Black Time, like his Mother, is beckoning him home
For now he must hibernate in the cell of his bedroom
And survive the tragic winter of his innate contradiction.

The Brother

On St John's night
I went out for a walk
At 9 p.m.;
When I returned from my walk
At 3 a.m.
And saw the corpse of my brother
Spattered with blood
I stepped over it
And went to bed.

The next day I met my other brother
In the courtyard:
He said he had killed our brother
And I asked him why;
He said he thought he was a werewolf.

Well, I inherited the farm,
And that's the long and the short of it:
One brother murdered;
The other in jail for life;
And myself alone on the farm.

I am known locally as
'The brother'.

Birth of a Coachman

His father and grandfather before him were coachmen:
How strange, then, to think that this small, bloody, lump of flesh,
This tiny moneybags of brains, veins, and intestines,
This zipped-up purse of most peculiar coin,
Will one day be coachman of the Cork to Dublin route,
In a great black greatcoat and white gauntlets,
In full command of one of our famous coaches
— *Wonder, Perseverance, Diligence,* or *Lightning* —
In charge of all our lives on foul winter nights,
Crackling his whip, whirling it, lashing it,
Driving on the hapless horses across the moors
Of the Kilworth hills, beating them on
Across rivers in spate, rounding sharp bends
On only two wheels, shriekings of axle-trees,
Rock-scrapes, rut-squeals, quagmire-squelches,
For ever in dread of the pitiless highwayman
Lurking in ambush with a brace of pistols;
Then cantering carefully in the lee of the Galtees,
Bowing his head to the stone gods of Cashel;
Then again thrusting through Urlingford;
Doing his bit, and his nut, past the Devilsbit;
Praising the breasts of the hills round Port Laoise;
Sailing full furrow through the Curragh of Kildare,
Through the thousand sea-daisies of a thousand white sheep;
Thrashing gaily the air at first glimpse of the Liffey;
Until stepping down from his high perch in Dublin
Into the sanctuary of a cobbled courtyard,
Into the arms of a crowd like a triumphant toreador
All sweat and tears: the man of the moment
Who now is but a small body of but some fleeting seconds old.

Ireland 1977

'I've become so lonely, I could die' – he writes,
The native who is an exile in his native land:
'Do you hear me whispering to you across the Golden Vale?
Do you hear me bawling to you across the hearthrug?'

Fermoy Calling Moscow

Gunmen terrorise the tribe;
Parliamentarians dissemble and bribe;
Churchmice and churchmen scratch heaven;
But they'll not knock Mrs Crotty down.

She sells her sweetmeats and she makes her tea
And when things get bad on RTE
She tunes in to Radio Moscow while she irons:
O they'll not knock Mrs Crotty down.

Although the noise in Fermoy would make you brown
And the river floods houses in the rainy season
It's still not a bad old town:
O they'll not knock Mrs Crotty down.

On the wall of her lively room there's a sepia portrait
Of de Valera at a graveside and around her head his arm
When she was seven: through sorrow's smile he is about to state:
O they will never knock Mrs Crotty down.

Minister Opens New Home for Battered Husbands

The Minister for Justice wearing a new fur coat
Yesterday opened a home for battered husbands:
Present were leading farmers and greyhound-owners
As well as respectable solicitors with their mistresses.
While the Minister cut the tape to the new home
Several battered husbands could be seen cringing
On the staircase in tear-stained cardigans
And cracked slippers; and the stairs looked
As though they had received a liberal sprinkling
Of dandruff and cigarette ash. A spokesman for the husbands said:
We are relieved to have at last got a place of our own;
Several of the men are pregnant and the security
Which the new home will provide, is for them
A welcome boon. Asked as to what kind of injury
The husbands suffered from, the spokesman said that frayed nerves
Are the major ailment and further inspection revealed
Loose nerve-ends dangling from eye-sockets and cheek-bones.
It was also stated that in order to protect the men
From the wrath of their wives
A team of Limerick ban-gardaí – known as the heavy gang –
Will be on twenty-four-hour duty outside the new home.

The County Engineer

A tall heavy man with a short curly beard
He is a dragon on the site: bureaucrats quail
Before him, and gangers wince.
But in bed at night with his wife
She whispers to him
'Oh my little engineer.'
And she is tiny as a bird
And her black, sleek stilettos
Make her tiny legs bird-like
And her pointed breasts
Behind her red silk blouses
Are also bird-like
And her curled-up tongues
(Lizards in leaves)
And her pouncing eyes
(Tigers in cages)
Are veiled under wings
Of her long black tresses
Combed down to her thighs.
Her children think of her
As their favourite rag-doll
And few of her neighbours
Consider her real;
But at night in bed with her spouse
Grasping him between her knees
She whispers to him
'Oh my little engineer';
And being a practical creature
She has had an extra-large bath
Installed in the bathroom
For the bath is her favourite haunt
For the love-act
And immersed with her spouse
She whispers to him
'Oh my little engineer'.

Making Love outside Áras an Uachtaráin

When I was a boy, myself and my girl
Used bicycle up to the Phoenix Park;
Outside the gates we used lie in the grass
Making love outside Áras an Uachtaráin.

Often I wondered what de Valera would have thought
Inside in his ivory tower
If he knew that we were in his green, green grass
Making love outside Áras an Uachtaráin.

Because the odd thing was – oh how odd it was –
We both revered Irish patriots
And we dreamed our dreams of a green, green flag
Making love outside Áras an Uachtaráin.

But even had our names been Diarmaid and Gráinne
We doubted de Valera's approval
For a poet's son and a judge's daughter
Making love outside Áras an Uachtaráin.

I see him now in the heat-haze of the day
Blindly stalking us down;
And, levelling an ancient rifle, he says 'Stop
Making love outside Áras an Uachtaráin.'

The Most Beautiful Protestant Girl in Muggalnagrow

She wears hot pants and a skin-tight blouse
And we hear she is a demon at college – her divinity
Is simply first-class. Muggalnagrow men
Sit simply chatting in a rustic row
On stools outside their haunts on summer eves
Murmuring her name as she clops past,
Day-dreaming of marriage to her;
What jesse-trees take root, what exotic dynasties!
Her father is the local Presbyterian Minister
And he is mad about golf (except on Sundays
When his Catholic friends play four-balls:
He yearns to join-in in a four-ball:
The Lord God, why cannot he be in a four-ball?);
He is a left-hander and he has got a swing like a scythe;
He does not hit the ball – he mows it down.
But although he is mad about golf, he is madder
About his bogbrown, beanstalk daughter:
He cannot keep her away from young men
Nor young men away from sweet her; fifty-fifty
She will have a baby by one of them or, worse,
Marry him. Imagine having to suffer
One of those long-haired poetry-preaching goons
In my own living-room for the rest of my days?
O The Lord God, save me from distraction
Or I will have to resign my stipend of Muggalnagrow
And go die in an old, slated, home for elderly elders
Far from golf-courses and reality:
O my heavenly daughter, what about me?

Sister Agnes Writes to her Beloved Mother

Dear Mother, Thank you for the egg cosy;
Sister Alberta (from near Clonakilty)
Said it was the nicest, positively the nicest,
Egg cosy she had ever seen. Here
The big news is that Rev. Mother is pregnant;
The whole convent is simply delighted;
We don't know who the lucky father is
But we have a shrewd idea who it might be:
Do you remember that Retreat Director
I wrote to you about? – The lovely old Jesuit
With a rosy nose – We think it was he –
So shy and retiring, just the type;
Fr P.J. Pegasus S.J.
Of course, it's all hush-hush,
Nobody is supposed to know anything
In case the Bishop – that young hypocrite –
Might get to hear about it.
When her time comes Rev. Mother officially
Will go away on retreat
And the cherub will be reared in another convent.
But, considering the general decline in vocations,
We are all pleased as pea-shooters
That God has blessed the Order of the Little Tree
With another new sapling, all of our own making,
And of Jesuit pedigree, too.
Nevertheless – not a word.
Myself, I am crocheting a cradle-shawl;
Hope you're doing your novenas. Love, Aggie.

The Head Transplant

The doctor said to me: Your father needs a *new* head.
So I said to the doctor: You can give him *my* head.

My days were numbered – broken marriage, cancer,
False teeth, bad dreams – so 'Yes' was his answer.

Now I lie in my bed wondering away in my head
What will my father look like with his new head?

Will he look like a bull with the head of a daffodil
Or like a nonagenarian pontiff with the head of a harlot?

Or like a heavyweight weightlifter with the head of a fox
Or like a withered, agèd, tree with the sun in its branches?

My dreams and memories will percolate down his legs and arms;
My ideas will seep down his spine like the roots of a tree.

And my eyes will swivel in obeisance to their new rotator.
His friends will say: 'Quite remarkable the change in Old Harry –

His new head seems to be doing him the world of good.
Jolly lucky that blackguard son of his snuffed it when he did.'

And I, when I'm dead, will walk alone in the graveyard,
A ghost with no head, an authentic hobgoblin.

A truly real Irishman, a *giolla gan ceann*.

Irish Hierarchy Bans Colour Photography

After a Spring meeting in their nineteenth-century fastness at
    Maynooth
The Irish Hierarchy has issued a total ban on the practice of colour
    photography:
A spokesman added that while in accordance with tradition
No logical explanation would be provided
There were a number of illogical explanations which he would
    discuss;
He stated that it was not true that the ban was the result
Of the Hierarchy's tacit endorsement of racial discrimination;
(And, here, the spokesman, Fr Marksman, smiled to himself
But when asked to elaborate on his smile, he would not elaborate
Except to growl some categorical expletives which included the
    word 'liberal')
He stated that if the Press corps would countenance an unhappy pun
He would say that negative thinking lay at the root of the ban;
Colour pictures produced in the minds of people,
Especially in the minds (if any) of young people,
A serious distortion of reality;
Colour pictures showed reality to be rich and various
Whereas reality in point of fact was the opposite;
The innate black and white nature of reality would have to be
    safeguarded
At all costs and, talking of costs, said Fr Marksman,
It ought to be borne in mind, as indeed the Hierarchy had borne in its
    collective mind,
That colour photography was far costlier than black and white
    photography
And, as a consequence, more immoral;
The Hierarchy, stated Fr Marksman, was once again smiting two
    birds with one boulder;
And the joint-hegemony of Morality and Economics was being
    upheld.

The total ban came as a total surprise to the accumulated Press corps
And Irish Roman Catholic pressmen and presswomen present

Had to be helped away as they wept copiously in their cups:
'No more oranges and lemons in Maynooth' sobbed one cameraboy.
The general public, however, is expected to pay no heed to the ban;
Only politicians and time-servers are likely to pay the required
        lip-service;
But the operative noun is lip: there will be no hand or foot service.
And next year Ireland is expected to become
The EEC's largest money-spender in colour photography:

This is Claudia Conway RTE News (Colour) Maynooth.

Bishop of Cork Murders his Wife

Such is the loyalty of his flock
That on hearing that their bishop had murdered his wife
Their immediate response was not of sympathy for the deceased
But of regret that their bishop had ever got married:
Said one old-timer by the Lough
'He is a decent man -- he should have stayed single.'
And an old virago in a hood-cloak in the Glen descanted
'Oh the wicked trollop – oh the poor old boyo.'

The body of the deceased woman
Who in her teens was renowned as the Queen of Skibbereen
Was found underneath the Colour TV Set
In a hall in the west wing of the humble palace;
Apparently she had tried to prevent her husband
From watching 'Match Of The Day'.
Foolishly, and some would say sinfully,
She had wanted to spend the evening in a more intimate manner
Than watching a football match.

The couple had no children –
That were known of.

In latter years it had been well known
That his wife had long been a thorn
If not a spear
In the bishop's side:
Frequently she had embarrassed him
By chirping up for women's rights
And on more than one occasion
(The bishop was fond of regaling cronies
With tales of how his mother suckled him on porter)
When she had objected to his excessive drinking
He was heard to remonstrate with her
'You're not a patch on my mother
You skivvy you.'

The bishop will recuperate from this unfortunate incident
On an island loaned to him by a government minister;
Meanwhile the remains of his wife
Have been chucked into the River Lee;
There will be no funeral.

In Memory: The Miami Showband: Massacred 31 July 1975

Beautiful are the feet of them that preach the gospel of peace,
Of them that bring glad tidings of good things

In a public house, darkly-lit, a patriotic (sic)
Versifier whines into my face: 'You must take one side
Or the other, or you're but a fucking romantic.'
His eyes glitter hate and vanity, porter and whiskey,
And I realise that he is blind to the braille connection
Between a music and a music-maker.
'You must take one side or the other
Or you're but a fucking romantic':
The whine is icy
And his eyes hang loose like sheets from poles
On a bare wet hillside in winter
And his mouth gapes like a cave in ice;
It is a whine in the crotch of whose fear
Is fondled a dream-gun blood-smeared;
It is in war – not poetry or music –
That men find their niche, their glory hole;
Like most of his fellows
He will abide no contradiction in the mind:
He whines: 'If there is birth, there cannot be death'
And – jabbing a hysterical forefinger into my nose and eyes –
'If there is death, there cannot be birth.'
Peace to the souls of those who unlike my confrère
Were true to their trade
Despite death-dealing blackmail by racists:
You made music, and that was all: You were realists
And beautiful were your feet.

The Minibus Massacre: The Eve of the Epiphany

Ten men in a minibus
Glimpse a red torch
& are machine-gunned to bits,
Fleshrags and bloodrags:
The narrow mountain road
Strewn with corpses,
Slaughtered fish on a slipway,
Corpse upon corpse,
Workman upon workman,
Adorned with work's instruments –
Sandwich boxes and flasks,
Decks of playing cards.

In Armagh:
Ard Macha;
Altitudo Machae;
Height
Of Queen Macha;
The height of it;
The height of obscenity;
The green-clad lady
For whose liberty
We butcher.
After this night
In Armagh
Just after six
P.M.
Liberty in Ireland
Is a corpse:
And the graves of the 1916 leaders
Have been all dug up
By Irish-speaking Chicago-style gangsters
With names like Ó Brádaigh, Ó'Connaill;
And Pearse's skull used as a hurling ball
On O'Connell Street Bridge;

And John MacBride's shin-bones
Used to make hurling sticks
With which to whip-lash Pearse's skull
Up and down the bridge;
And gangs with evil of fear in their eyeslits
Hissing: We're off to Dublin in the green, in the green.

Oh, this night our ballads taste far richer
Than any high-born traitor's horse-manure
And tomorrow at breakfast
        – Epiphany of Epiphanies –
The heroic leaders of the IRA
Will crouch down to chew sausages,
Planting them carefully between their lips.

5 January 1976

National Day of Mourning for 12 Protestants

Throughout the Republic of Ireland yesterday
A National Day of Mourning was observed
For the 12 Protestant dog-lovers and junior motor-cyclists
Who were burnt to death last Friday night
At the La Mon House Restaurant in Comber, Co. Down,
By a gang of Republican Assassins.
In Dublin the Taoiseach, Mr Jack Lynch,
Together with the Roman Catholic Archbishop of Armagh, Dr
    Ó Fíaich
Led a Vigil of Mourning
Outside the Kevin Street headquarters of the Republican Terrorists.
A symbolic fire was lit
And both the Taoiseach and the Archbishop
Joined together as one man
And blew it out with one breath.
The Vigil concluded with the momentous announcement
That Mrs Mairín Lynch, wife of the Taoiseach,
Was to forgo a crucial week of fête-openings
In order to make the twelve-hour train journey to Belfast
At the invitation of the Peace People.
Later the GIS (the Government Information Services)
Denied rumours that the principals at the Vigil of Mourning
Were impostors and that the real Dr Ó Fíaich,
Together with the real Mr and Mrs Lynch,
Were attending a Gaelic football match somewhere in Corkery.
Government officials stated that reality did not enter into the matter.

February 1978

Margaret Thatcher Joins IRA

At a ritual ceremony in a fairy ring fort
Near Bodenstown Graveyard, Co. Kildare
(Burial place of Theobald Wolfe Tone)
Margaret Thatcher joined the IRA
And the IRA joined Margaret Thatcher.

Black dresses were worn by all for the occasion
In which a historical union was consummated.

On the circular bank of the rath
Gunmen and High Tories crawled on all fours
Jangling their testicles;
While the sun gleamed off their buttocks.

At the navel of the rath
Waltzed Ruarí Ó Brádaigh,
His arms round Mrs Thatcher
In a sweet embrace.
Behind them Messrs
Airey Neave & Daithí O'Connell
Shared a seat on a pig.

Proceedings concluded
With Sir Ó Brádaigh, an Thatcher, an Neave, agus Sir O'Connell
Playing cops and robbers in souterrains.

Meanwhile in his leaba (his grave)
In nearby Bodenstown
Theobald Wolfe Tone was to be observed
Revolving sixty revolutions per minute;
This came as no surprise to observers
Since Tone was a thoroughgoing dissenter
And never would have had truck
With the likes of Margaret Thatcher or the IRA.

February 1978

In Memoriam Seamus Murphy:
October 1975

It is deserted today in the municipal park;
Deserted swing and slide, deserted path and riverbank;
Yet, the more deserted the municipal park by the river,
The more life-like transpires the *Virgin of the Twilight*.

'What is a sculpture, Daddy?'
A small girl inquires of her father
Meandering through the municipal park;
He indicates a statue
Named *Virgin of the Twilight;*
He stoops down and he explains:
'That was made by a man called Seamus Murphy –
It is a sculpture.'

The daughter stares up at the madonna and baby
Carved in white limestone;
The father stares down at the daughter transfixed
By the puzzle of birth;
Knowing that one bleak day she also will be
Alone in the world – desolate in the park –
Bereft, lit, creased, soaked, scourged
By wind, rain, sunlight, snow.

'Where is Seamus Murphy now?'
Yelled the small girl turning upwards her eyes:
'He has gone home to. . .' stammered the father
'And. . .' – and, as he groped for language,
She intervened as if already having arrived at
A final, restful, and most satisfactory conclusion:
'He has left behind him his sculpture, Daddy.'

The sculpture remains:
Father after daughter
Disappear off –
Into the vanishing light.

Lament for Major-General Emmet Dalton

to Cathal O'Shannon

The gun-carriage bearing your coffin
Trundled unnoticed through Dublin streets:
The mob, in tune with the mobsters,
Disowned you, Emmet Dalton;
Disremembering Michael Collins also
Whom you held in your trembling arms
As he lay dying at the Mouth of Flowers.

At Glasnevin Cemetery, a firing party
Fired over your grave their hollow volleys:
No one noticed except God in his heaven
If there be a heaven – which for military men
Like yourself must seem most improbable:
The next life was cradling the head of your dying comrade,
Blood cascading from huge Japanese waterfall behind earlobe.

When civil war arrived at the pit of degradation
With fiats of summary executions,
And revenge and counter-revenge assumed their sway,
You resigned from the army; in the post-war scramble
For dividing-up the lolly, you kept well out of it,
Preferring the art of film-making (a new art in Ireland)
To that old Celtic game – Tammany Hall politics.

You who first saw service in the Great War
(O what made it Great? O save us O Lord from Greatness)
Treaded the trenches whose bottoms were floored
With the caked-up bones of the six-months-dead;
You were twenty, then, a moustachio'd young captain
Dreaming of deeds of derring-do; instead, you had the privilege
Of seeing Tom Kettle having his head blown off on the road to
     Guinchy.

Sixty years later you revisited those pastoral scenes
Of that most dreadful carnage; they were as unrecognisable

As the nearby dales of white crosses to the anonymous dead:
You leaned back on your stick, gazed out through your spectacles;
Sadly and gracefully, bewildered and bemused:
At the Mouth of Flowers you re-enacted the Ambush –
Yet the deed remained as sinister as the location itself.

Now, Emmet Dalton, you, also, are part of the clay;
Crocodile worms and rhinoceros slugs advance on their prey;
What are we left with? At dusk, on the River Lee, a steamer
Steams out to sea with a dead King's coffin on board,
And, beside it, keeping guard, the dead King's young friend;
Whose habit was truth, and whose style was courage.

March 1978

100

Micheál Mac Liammóir

'Dear Boy, What a superlative day for a funeral:
It seems St Stephen's Green put on the appareil
Of early Spring-time especially for me.
That is no vanity: but – dare I say it – humility
In the fell face of those nay-neighers who say we die
At dying-time. Die? Why, I must needs cry
No, no, no, no,
Now I am living whereas before – no –
'Twas but breathing, choking, croaking, singing,
Superb sometimes but nevertheless but breathing:
You should have seen the scene in University Church:
Packed to the hammer-beams with me left in the lurch
All on my ownio up-front centre-stage;
People of every nationality in Ireland and of every age;
Old age and youth – Oh, everpresent, oldest, wished-for youth;
And old Dublin ladies telling their beads for old me; forsooth.
'Twould have fired the cockles of John Henry's heart
And his mussels too: only Sara Bernhardt
Was missing but I was so glad to see Marie Conmee
Fresh, as always, as the morning sea.
We paid a last farewell to dear Harcourt Terrace,
Dear old, bedraggled, doomed Harcourt Terrace
Where I enjoyed, amongst the crocuses, a Continual Glimpse of
            Heaven
By having, for a living partner, Hilton.
Around the corner the canal-waters from Athy gleamed
Engaged in their never-ending courtship of Ringsend.
Then onward to the Gate – and to the rose-cheeked ghost of Lord
            Edward Longford;
I could not bear to look at Patrick Bedford.
Oh tears there were, there and everywhere,
But especially there; there outside the Gate where
For fifty years we wooed the goddess of our art;
How many, many nights she pierced my heart.
Ach, níl aon tinteán mar do thinteán féin:
The Gate and the *Taibhdhearc* – each was our name;

I dreamed a dream of Jean Cocteau
Leaning against a wall in Killnamoe;
And so I voyaged through all the nations of Ireland with McMaster
And played in Cinderella an ugly, but oh so ugly, sister.
Ah but we could not tarry for ever outside the Gate;
Life, as always, must go on or we'd be late
For my rendezvous with my brave grave-diggers
Who were as shy but snappy as my best of dressers.
We sped past the vast suburb of Clontarf – all those lives
Full of hard-working Brian Borús with their busy wives.
In St Fintan's Cemetery there was spray from the sea
As well as from the noonday sun, and clay on me:
And a green carnation on my lonely oaken coffin.
Lonely in heaven? Yes, I must not soften
The deep pain I feel at even a momentary separation
From my dear, sweet friends. A green carnation
For you all, dear boy; If you must weep, ba(w)ll;
Slán agus Beannacht: Micheál.'

March 1978

Lament for Cearbhall Ó Dálaigh

Into a simple grave six feet deep,
Next grave to a Kerry sheep farmer,
Your plain oak coffin was laid
In a hail of hail:
The gods in the Macgillycuddy's Reeks
(Snow on their summits)
Were in a white, dancing rage
Together with the two don-
Keys who would not budge
From the graveyard,
And the poets and the painters,
The actors and the actresses,
The etchers and the sculptors,
The child-singers – those multiplying few
Who, despite the ever-darkening night,
Believe with their hearts' might
As did you
In a spoken music of the utter earth:

You who, for a brief hour,
Were Chieftain of a Rising People;
Who brought back into Tara's Halls
The blind poets and the blinder harpists;
Who, the brief hour barely ended,
Were insulted massively,
Betrayed
By a monstrous bourgeoisie;
And, worse by far,
By *la trahaison des clercs;*
Where were those talented men
In the government of the talents
When the jackbooted
Bourgeois crackled the whip?
The talented men kept their silence,
Their souls committed to finance;
Now hear their mouth-traps snap shut:
'No comment, no comment, no comment, no comment.'

Ah, Cearbhall, but in your death
You led them all a merry dance:
Hauling them all out of their soft Dublin haunts,
Out of their Slickness and Glickness,
Out of their Snugvilles and Smugtowns,
You had them travel all the long,
Long way down to Sneem:
Sneem of the Beautiful Knot:
By God, and By Dana,
Cearbhall, forgive me
But it was a joy to watch them
With their wind-flayed faces
Getting all knotted-up
In the knot of your funeral;
Wind, rain, hail, and sleet,
Were on your side;
And spears of sunlight
Who, like yourself, did not lie;
Blue Lightning –
And Thunder inscribed on the mountaintops;
And Disgrace on the faces.

In all our memories, Cearbhall,
You will remain as fresh
As the green rock jutting up
In mid-stream
Where fresh and salt waters meet
Under the Bridge at Sneem.

How the respectability squirmed
In the church when beside your coffin
The Ó Riada choir sang pagan laments
For their dead chieftain:
'O he is my hero, my brave loved one.'
Papal Nuncio, Bishops, Monsignori,
Passed wind in their misericords,
Their stony faces expressionless.
A Gaelic Chinaman whose birthplace
At 85 Main Street, Bray,

104

Is today a Chinese Restaurant
('The Jasmine' owned by Chi Leung Nam);
O tan-man smiling on the mountain,
You are gone from us now, O Yellow Sun:
Small laughing man,
Cearbhall of the merry eyes,
A Gaelic Charlie Chaplin who became
Chief Justice and President,
Hear our mute confessions now:
We were afraid of the man that licks
Life with such relish;
We were not up to your tricks,
Did not deserve you, Cearbhall
Of the City-Centre and the Mountain-Pool:
Príomh Breitheamh, Uachtarán: Slán.

March 1978

The Drimoleague Blues
for Sarah and Síabhra

Oh I know this mean town is not always mean
And I know that you do not always mean what you mean
And the meaning of meaning can both mean and not mean:
But I mean to say; I mean to say;
I've got the Drimoleague Blues, I've got the Drimoleague Blues,
I've got the Drimoleague Blues so bad I can't move:
Even if you were to plug in Drimoleague to every oil-well in Arabia –
I'd still have the Drimoleague Blues.

Oh this town is so mean that it's got its own mean
And that's to be as mean as green, as mean as green:
Shoot a girl dead and win yourself a bride,
Shoot a horse dead and win yourself a car:
Oh I've got the Drimoleague Blues, I've got the Drimoleague Blues,
I've got the Drimoleague Blues so bad I can't move:
Even if you were to plug in Drimoleague to every oil-well in Arabia –
I'd still have the Drimoleague Blues.

And so on right down to the end of the line
Mean with Mean will always rhyme
And Man with Man: Oh, where is the Woman
With the Plough, where is her Daughter with the Stars?
Oh I've got the Drimoleague Blues, I've got the Drimoleague Blues,
I've got the Drimoleague Blues so bad I can't move:
Even if you were to plug in Drimoleague to every oil-well in Arabia –
I'd still have the Drimoleague Blues.

Sally

Sally, I was happy with *you*.

Yet a dirty cafeteria in a railway station –
In the hour before dawn over a formica table
Confetti'ed with cigarette ash and coffee stains –
Was all we ever knew of a home together.

'Give me a child and let me go.'
'Give me a child and let me stay.'
She to him and he to her;
Which said *which*? and *who* was *who*?

Sally, I was happy with *you*.

That Propeller I Left in Bilbao

Would you like a whiskey? Good:
That's my girl: how I do like to see
You with a glass of whiskey in your hand,
And that gleam of a smile beneath your hat:

And that gleam of a smile beneath your hat:
But that propeller I left in Bilbao –
I ought to tell you about it now –
But, blast it, I won't; let's have a row:

Ow: Ow: Ow: let's have a row:
Let's pink the pink floor pinker than pink:
I am a pink place in which a pink pig plashes:
You are a pink peach in which a pink babe perishes –

Perishes to be born! Put in a new cassette!
And let the cherry-blossom blossom till it fall
Asunder – Oh my Pink Thunder – asunder
And that propeller I left in Bilbao

Is still that propeller I left in Bilbao;
But you have sheared off all your clothes
And you would like, if it pleases me, a second whiskey:
Why of course, my Big Pink Thunderbird –

My Big Pink Thunderbird – why of course –
Do you know how many telephone calls I had today?
The flaming phone never stopped flaming ringing
And all about that propeller I left in Bilbao:

All about that propeller I left in Bilbao:
I said: 'Telex' to them all: 'Telex':
And now to you, love, Telex Forever and Forever Telex,
And may that propeller I left in Bilbao

Well – may that propeller I left in Bilbao –
That propeller I left in Bilbao –
Propeller I left in Bilbao –
I left in Bilbao.

The Daughter Finds her Father Dead

for A.D.

The day that Father died
I went up to wake him at 8.30 a.m.
Before I left home for school:
The night before he had said
Before I went up to bed
'Remember to wake me at 8.30 a.m.
Remember to wake me at 8.30 a.m.'

The day that Father died
At 8.30 a.m. I went up to wake him
And I thought at first he was dead:
He did not move when I shook him:
But then he said, then he said
'Rider Haggard, Rider Haggard:
Storm Jameson, Storm Jameson'.

The day that Father died
Those were the last words he said:
'Rider Haggard, Rider Haggard:
Storm Jameson, Storm Jameson'.
I thought then he was alive
But he was dead, he was dead;
When I came from school he was dead.

The day that Father died
I glimpsed him telescopically:
Inside in his eyes inside in his head
A small voice in a faraway world
Spinning like a tiny coin:
'Rider Haggard, Rider Haggard:
Storm Jameson, Storm Jameson'.

Apparently – I suppose I should say
'It seems' – Father was a man
Who thought God was a woman

And that was why he was always sad,
Bad at being glad:
'Rider Haggard, Rider Haggard:
Storm Jameson, Storm Jameson'.

He cries and he cries, over and over,
In the empty nights that are emptier
And the dark days that are darker:
'Rider Haggard, Rider Haggard:
Storm Jameson, Storm Jameson':
And I take a look out from my bunk bed
As if all the world were a black silhouette

Or an infinite series of black silhouettes
Brokenly riding the white skyline:
'Rider Haggard, Rider Haggard:
Storm Jameson, Storm Jameson':
And just as my father thought God was a woman
I think God is a man: are both of us wrong?
Oh if only a horse could write a song:

Oh if only a horse could write a song.

Hopping round Knock Shrine in the Falling Rain: 1958

to Karol Wojtyla

When I was thirteen I broke my leg.

Being the sensible, superstitious old lady that she was,
My Aunt Sarah knew that, while to know God was good,
To get the Ear of his Mother was a more practical step:
Kneeling on the flagstone floor of her kitchen, all teaspoons and
    whins,
Outspoken as Moses, she called out Litanies to Our Lady:
The trick was to circumambulate the Shrine fifteen times
Repeating the rosary, telling your beads
And so: that is how I came to be
Hopping round Knock Shrine in the Falling Rain.

In the Heel of that Spritual Hunt
I became a Falling Figure clinging to the Shrine Wall
While Mayo rain pelleted down jamming and jetting:
And, while all the stalls – of relics, and phials of holy water,
And souvenir grottos, and souvenir postcards,
And spheres which, when shaken, shook with fairy snow,
And sticks of Knock Rock –
Were being folded up for the day, I veered on
Falling round Knock Shrine in the Hopping Rain.

Gable, O Gable, is there no Respite to thy Mercy?

The trick did not work
But that is scarcely the point:
That day was a crucial day
In my hedge school of belief
In the Potential of Miracle,
In the Actuality of Vision:
And, therefore, I am grateful
For my plateful
Of Hopping round Knock Shrine in the Falling Rain.

Tullynoe: Tête-à-Tête in the Parish Priest's Parlour

'Ah, he was a grand man.'
'He was: he fell out of the train going to Sligo.'
'He did: he thought he was going to the lavatory.'
'He did: in fact he stepped out the rear door of the train.'
'He did: God, he must have got an awful fright.'
'He did: he saw that it wasn't the lavatory at all.'
'He did: he saw that it was the railway tracks going away from him.'
'He did: I wonder if. . . but he was a grand man.'
'He was: he had the most expensive Toyota you can buy.'
'He had: well, it was only beautiful.'
'He had: he used to have an Audi.'
'He had: as a matter of fact he used to have two Audis.'
'He had: and then he had an Avenger.'
'He had: and then he had a Volvo.'
'He had: in the beginning he had a lot of Volkses.'
'He had: he was a great man for the Volkses.'
'He was: did he once have an Escort?'
'He had not: he had a son a doctor.'
'He had: and he had a Morris Minor too.'
'He had: he had a sister a hairdresser in Killmallock.'
'He had: he had another sister a hairdresser in Ballybunnion.'
'He had: he was put in a coffin which was put in his father's cart.'
'He was: his ladywife sat on top of the coffin driving the donkey.'
'She did: Ah but he was a grand man.'
'He was: he was a grand man. . .'
'Goodnight, Father.'
'Goodnight, Mary.'

Charlie's Mother

Brendan, does *your* mother have a hold over *you*?
Mine does over *me*. I keep beseeching her
To take her purple-veined hand out of my head
But do you know what she says, the old cabbage?
Stirring and churning her hand round inside in my head
She crows: Charlie m'boy, you've got a lot of neck.

Mind you, when I think about it, she has a point:
My neck *is* thick and there *is* rather a lot of it;
And look at all the *mun* I have made
Without having to do a flick of work for it.
I rub my neck wryly when Mother crows:
That's m'boy Charlie, lots of *mun* for *mum*.

And you know, Brendan – would you like another drink?
Double brandy there please – I often think, Brendan,
When I look at myself in the mirror each morning –
And I must admit that that's my favourite moment of each day –
Even on black bloody days like today – I always see
Somewhere behind my fat neck my tiny little mother winking up at
      me.

Another drink? Certainly Brendan. Double brandy there please.
Down, Bismarck, down. Down, Bismarck, down.
Damned Alsatian bitch but a friendly bitch at heart;
Mother gave her to me as a Christian – I mean Christmas – present.
Another drink? Certainly Brendan, quadruple brandy there please.
Down, Bismarck, down. Down, Bismarck, down.

But, Brendan, you were saying about Micky Finn of Castlepollard
That his mother has run away and left him for another man?
Another case, I'm afraid, of not keeping the hand in the till;
Not enough neck at all at all. Can you hear me, Brendan?
Come on, a Mhic, straighten up for Christ's sake – or at least for
      Ireland's sake.
Down, Bismarck, down. Down, Bismarck, down.

Brendan, do you realise, you pixillated, feckless sot
That if my mother came in here just now as she might very well do
(Mothers tend to eavesdrop in the footsteps of their favourite
          offspring)
She might think that I am to blame for the condition you're in:
You're not just drunk – you're in a coma:
She might even decide to turn Bismarck against me.

Eat him, Bismarck, eat him.
      Eat him, Bismarck, eat him.

Nyum: nyum, nyum, nyum, nyum, nyum; Nyum.

The Man whose Name was Tom-and-Ann

When you enter a room where there is a party in progress
Normally you ignore the introductions:
This is Tom; and Jerry; and Micky; and Mouse –
They are all much the same – male mouths
Malevolent with magnanimity or females
Grinning gratuitously: but tonight
I paid attention when I was introduced to a man
Whose name was Tom-and-Ann:
All night I looked hard at him from all angles,
Even going so far as to look down his brass neck,
But all I could see was a young, middle-aged man
With coal-black hair cut in a crew-cut such
As would make you freeze, or faint, of electric shock:
Nobody had noticed that his wife was not with him:
She was at another party being introduced to *my* wife
Who, when she came home, started humming
'Tonight I met a woman whose name was Ann-and-Tom.'

Well, next time I throw a party for all the Foleys in Ireland,
God help us, I will do the introductions myself:
'Darling Donal, – This is Tom-and-Ann
And his beautiful wife Ann-and-Tom.'

En Famille, 1979

Bring me back to the dark school – to the dark school of childhood:
To where tiny is tiny, and massive is massive.

Madman

Every child has a madman on their street:
The only trouble about *our* madman is that he's our father.

My 27 Psychiatrists

I keep the 27 psychiatrists whom I own under the bed:
I go to sleep on the couch to the rapturous song of their howling.

Maimie

There in the river I saw her body:
Was it Maimie? Who else could it be?

On Seeing Two Bus Conductors Kissing Each Other in the Middle of the Street

Electricity zig-zags through me into the blue leatherette
And I look around quick and yes –
All faces are in a state of shock:
By Christ, – this busride
Will be the busride to beat all busrides.

Sure enough the conductor comes waltzing up the stairs –
The winding stairs –
And he comes up the aisle a-hopping and a-whooping
So I take my chance
Being part of the dance:
I say: 'A penny please.'
'Certainly, Sir' he replies
And rummages in his satchel
Until he fishes out a tiny penny,
An eenshy-weenshy penny,
Which he hands me crooning –
'That's especially for you Sir – thank you, Sir,'

So there it is, or was:
Will the day or night ever come when I will see
Two policemen at a street corner caressing each other?
Let the prisoners escape, conceal them in a sunbeam?
O my dear Guard William, O my darling Guard John.

For My Lord Tennyson I Shall Lay Down My Life

for Anthony Cronin

Here at the Mont St Michel of my master,
At the horn of beaches outside Locksley Hall,
On the farthest and coldest shore,
In the June day under pain of night,
I keep at my mind to make it say,
Make it say, make it say,
As his assassins make for me,
The pair of them revolving nearer and nearer
(And yet, between breaths, farther and farther),
Make it say:
'For My Lord Tennyson I Shall Lay Down My Life.'

I say that – as nearer and nearer they goosetep:
Vanity: and *Gloom* not far behind.
'For My Lord Tennyson I Shall Lay Down My Life.'

The Death by Heroin of Sid Vicious

There – but for the clutch of luck – go I.

At daybreak – in the arctic fog of a February
     daybreak –
Shoulderlength helmets in the watchtowers of the
     concentration camp
Caught me out in the intersecting arcs of the
     swirling searchlights:

There were at least a zillion of us caught out there
– Like   ladybirds   under   a   boulder   –
But under the microscope each of us was unique,

Unique and we broke for cover, crazily breasting
The barbed wire and some of us made it
To the forest edge, but many of us did not

Make it, although their unborn children did –
Such as you whom the camp commandant branded
Sid Vicious of the Sex Pistols. Jesus, break his fall:

There – but for the clutch of luck – go we all.

February 1979

NOTES

p. 16 *buachaillín*: small boy.
p. 31 *scoraíocht*: visiting neighbours for festive gossip.
p. 30 *Boyle Somerville:* On 24 March 1936, at his home in Castletownsend, Co. Cork, Admiral Boyle Somerville was murdered by the IRA.
p. 63 *crannóg:* lake-dwelling.
p. 85 *Áras an Uachtaráin*: The President's Mansion.
p. 88 *giolla gan ceann*: fellow without a head
p. 101 *Ach, níl aon tinteán mar do thinteán féin*: There's no place like home.
Taibhdhearc: the Theatre
p. 102 *Slán agus Beannacht*: Farewell and bless you.
p. 105 *Príomh Breitheamh, Uachtarán: Slán*: Chief Justice, President: Farewell.

Index of Titles

Index of First Lines

124

POETS FROM THE NORTH OF IRELAND
edited by Frank Ormsby

GEORGE BUCHANAN
CIARÁN CARSON
GERALD DAWE
SEAMUS DEANE
PADRAIC FIACC
MICHAEL FOLEY
SEAMUS HEANEY
JOHN HEWITT
MICHAEL LONGLEY
ROY McFADDEN
LOUIS MACNEICE
DEREK MAHON
TOM MATTHEWS
JOHN MONTAGUE
PAUL MULDOON
FRANK ORMSBY
TOM PAULIN
WILLIAM PESKETT
W.R. RODGERS
JAMES SIMMONS

'*full of exquisite verbal pleasures*' **Birmingham Post**

'*It is a duty of the poet to defend private values in a time of public clamour, and one of the unexpected strengths of this anthology is its selection of love poems.*' **TLS**

'*The richness which has resulted from the merging of two traditions is amply demonstrated in this splendid anthology*' **Sunday Independent**

'*a rich and representative collection*' **School Librarian**

ISBN 0 85640 201 X hb £6.50
ISBN 0 85640 135 8 pb £3.95

THE YOUNGER IRISH POETS
edited by Gerald Dawe

PAUL DURCAN
EAVAN BOLAND
RICHARD RYAN
MICHAEL FOLEY
HUGH MAXTON
PAUL MURRAY
FRANK ORMSBY
CIARÁN CARSON
TOM PAULIN
PATRICK WILLIAMS
MEDBH McGUCKIAN
PETER FALLON
ROBERT JOHNSTONE
PAUL MULDOON
GERARD SMYTH
HARRY CLIFTON
GERALD DAWE
WILLIAM PESKETT
MATTHEW SWEENEY
THOMAS McCARTHY
AIDAN CARL MATHEWS

The first anthology devoted to the poetry written by Irish poets born since the mid 1940s. These poets represent an impressive range of experience and literary styles. Their move away from a burdensome past, testing the limits of society, makes Irish poetry more open and diverse than it has ever been, and suggests that a literature which has changed the course of writing in English during this century has an exciting future.

'an excellent synoptic view of the possibilities of Irish poetry in the present moment. . . I'd hope that enlightened second-level teachers of English in Northern and Southern Ireland would smuggle it over the borders of whatever curricula they're supposed to live within.'
Irish Times

ISBN 0 85640 261 3 pb £4.95